TWINSBURG LIBRARY
TWINSBURG OHIO 44087

Xavier University
Cincinnati, Ohio

Written by David Gilmore

Edited by Adam Burns, Kelly Carey, Kimberly Moore, and Jon Skindzier

Layout by Adam Burns

Additional contributions by Omid Gohari, Christina Koshzow, Chris Mason, Joey Rahimi, and Luke Skurman

D1379355

ISBN # 1-4274-0222-1
ISSN # 1552-1869
© Copyright 2006 College Prowler
All Rights Reserved
Printed in the U.S.A.
www.collegeprowler.com

✓ISBN
YA 378.73
Gil

Last updated: 05/15/06

Special Thanks To: Babs Carryer, Andy Hannah, LaunchCyte, Tim O'Brien, Bob Sehlinger, Thomas Emerson, Andrew Skurman, Barbara Skurman, Bert Mann, Dave Lehman, Daniel Fayock, Chris Babyak, The Donald H. Jones Center for Entrepreneurship, Terry Slease, Jerry McGinnis, Bill Ecenberger, Idie McGinty, Kyle Russell, Jacque Zaremba, Larry Winderbaum, Roland Allen, Jon Reider, Team Evankovich, Lauren Varacalli, Abu Noaman, Mark Exler, Daniel Steinmeyer, Jared Cohon, Gabriela Oates, David Koegler, and Glen Meakem.

Bounce-Back Team: Jimmy Dillon, Wayler Envik, and Dan Cox.

College Prowler®
5001 Baum Blvd.
Suite 750
Pittsburgh, PA 15213

Phone: 1-800-290-2682
Fax: 1-800-772-4972
E-Mail: info@collegeprowler.com
Web Site: www.collegeprowler.com

College Prowler® is not sponsored by, affiliated with, or approved by Xavier University in any way.

College Prowler® strives faithfully to record its sources. As the reader understands, opinions, impressions, and experiences are necessarily personal and unique. Accordingly, there are, and can be, no guarantees of future satisfaction extended to the reader.

© Copyright 2006 College Prowler. All rights reserved. No part of this work may be reproduced or transmitted in any form or by any means, including but not limited to, photocopy, recording, or any information storage and retrieval systems, without the express written permission of College Prowler®.

Welcome to College Prowler®

During the writing of College Prowler's guidebooks, we felt it was critical that our content was unbiased and unaffiliated with any college or university. We think it's important that our readers get honest information and a realistic impression of the student opinions on any campus—that's why if any aspect of a particular school is terrible, we (unlike a campus brochure) intend to publish it. While we do keep an eye out for the occasional extremist—the cheerleader or the cynic—we take pride in letting the students tell it like it is. We strive to create a book that's as representative as possible of each particular campus. Our books cover both the good and the bad, and whether the survey responses point to recurring trends or a variation in opinion, these sentiments are directly and proportionally expressed through our guides.

College Prowler guidebooks are in the hands of students throughout the entire process of their creation. Because you can't make student-written guides without the students, we have students at each campus who help write, randomly survey their peers, edit, layout, and perform accuracy checks on every book that we publish. From the very beginning, student writers gather the most up-to-date stats, facts, and inside information on their colleges. They fill each section with student quotes and summarize the findings in editorial reviews. In addition, each school receives a collection of letter grades (A through F) that reflect student opinion and help to represent contentment, prominence, or satisfaction for each of our 20 specific categories. Just as in grade school, the higher the mark the more content, more prominent, or more satisfied the students are with the particular category.

Once a book is written, additional students serve as editors and check for accuracy even more extensively. Our bounce-back team—a group of randomly selected students who have no involvement with the project—are asked to read over the material in order to help ensure that the book accurately expresses every aspect of the university and its students. This same process is applied to the 200-plus schools College Prowler currently covers. Each book is the result of endless student contributions, hundreds of pages of research and writing, and countless hours of hard work. All of this has led to the creation of a student information network that stretches across the nation to every school that we cover. It's no easy accomplishment, but it's the reason that our guides are such a great resource.

When reading our books and looking at our grades, keep in mind that every college is different and that the students who make up each school are not uniform—as a result, it is important to assess schools on a case-by-case basis. Because it's impossible to summarize an entire school with a single number or description, each book provides a dialogue, not a decision, that's made up of 20 different topics and hundreds of student quotes. In the end, we hope that this guide will serve as a valuable tool in your college selection process. Enjoy!

OMID GOHARI ○ CHRISTINA KOSHZOW ○ CHRIS MASON ○ JOEY RAHIMI ○ LUKE SKURMAN ○
The College Prowler Team

Table of Contents

By the Numbers............................ **1**

Academics **4**

Local Atmosphere **11**

Safety & Security **17**

Computers................................. **22**

Facilities..................................... **28**

Campus Dining.......................... **33**

Off-Campus Dining **39**

Campus Housing....................... **46**

Off-Campus Housing................ **53**

Diversity..................................... **57**

Guys & Girls............................... **62**

Athletics..................................... **68**

Nightlife..................................... **74**

Greek Life **83**

Drug Scene................................ **86**

Campus Strictness **91**

Parking....................................... **95**

Transportation **100**

Weather................................... **106**

Report Card Summary **110**

Overall Experience **111**

The Inside Scoop.................... **114**

Finding a Job or Internship **118**

Alumni **120**

Student Organizations........... **123**

The Best & Worst.................... **129**

Visiting..................................... **131**

Words to Know........................ **136**

Introduction from the Author

"Zayvier," "Ecks-avier," or just plain "X." Whatever you choose to call Xavier University, there are roughly 4,000 young minds who call it home. Xavier may be known nationally for its past successes in the NCAA men's basketball tournament, but contrary to popular belief, there is life here outside of March.

We live in an age of hybrids. People drive gas/electric cars, we go see movies by writer/directors, and some of the most talented players in the NBA are guard/forwards. Xavier represents another dynamic combination in our society with its small school/big school mentality. As paradoxical as it may seem, after reading this guide, I hope you'll understand what I'm talking about.

Situated in Cincinnati on the Ohio River, Xavier is a small Jesuit Catholic college by classification, and a burgeoning university by observation. Confused yet? Let me try and explain. Xavier has everything you'd want from a large state school: top-notch facilities, academic prestige, hi-tech equipment, shiny new buildings, and nationally-competitive sports teams. However, what is not lost in all the bells and whistles of a major university is the tight-knit campus community that is Xavier.

When I go to visit my friends at their large state schools, I often wonder if they ever see the same person twice in a week. Here at Xavier, you have the opportunity to get to know all kinds of people in a multitude of different settings—whether it be in the classroom, at a party, or at a basketball game—it is assured that you are going to meet some amazing people.

When I was looking at schools to attend, the only thing I could tell you about Xavier was that they were a good basketball school, and that it was somewhere out in the Midwest. After reading all the literature the University sent me, the only new knowledge I had gained was that it was the "most magical place on earth." They have some good people working in the University Relations Department. Anyway, my point is that you can never tell about a school until you first visit it, and then talk to everyone you can who goes there. Personally, I didn't talk to enough people or read enough about the school before I came here, but luckily, it was the right choice for me. The idea behind this book is that where you go to school is an important decision—too important to leave up to the brochures and public opinion. Hopefully, this guide will get you started in finding out if you want to spend the next four years of your life at a place like Xavier.

David Gilmore, Author
Xavier University

By the Numbers

General Information

Xavier University
3800 Victory Parkway
Cincinnati, OH 45207

Control:
Private

Academic Calendar:
Semester

Religious Affiliation:
Roman Catholic (Jesuit)

Founded:
1831

Web Site:
www.xavier.edu

Main Phone:
(513) 745-3000

Admissions Phone:
(513) 745-3301

Student Body

**Full-Time
Undergraduates:**
3,365

**Part-Time
Undergraduates:**
578

**Total Male
Undergraduates:**
1,735

**Total Female
Undergraduates:**
2,208

Admissions

Overall Acceptance Rate:
74%

Total Applicants:
4,764

Total Acceptances:
3,519

Freshman Enrollment:
878

Yield (% of admitted students who actually enroll):
18%

Early Decision Available?
No

Early Action Available?
No

Regular Decision Deadline:
February 1

Must-Reply-By Date:
May 1

Applicants Placed on Waiting List:
149

Applicants Accepted from Waiting List:
43

Students Enrolled from Waiting List:
2

Transfer Applications Received:
357

Transfer Applications Accepted:
161

Transfer Students Enrolled:
82

Transfer Application Acceptance Rate:
23%

Common Application Accepted?
Yes

Supplemental Forms?
Yes

Admissions E-Mail:
xuadmit@xavier.edu

Admissions Web Site:
www.xu.edu/admission

SAT I or ACT Required?
Either

SAT I Range (25th–75th Percentile):
1060–1290

SAT I Verbal Range (25th–75th Percentile):
530–640

SAT I Math Range (25th–75th Percentile):
530–650

Freshmen Retention Rate:
89%

→

**Top 10% of
High School Class:**
29%

Application Fee:
$35

Financial Information

Tuition and Fees:
$21,830

Students Who Received Aid:
50%

Room and Board:
$8,060

Financial Aid Forms Deadline:
February 15

Books and Supplies:
$900

Financial Aid Phone:
(513) 745-3142

**Average Need-Based
Financial Aid Package
(including loans, work-study,
grants, and other sources):**
$13,874

Financial Aid E-Mail:
xufinaid@xu.edu

Financial Aid Web Site:
www.xavier.edu/financial_aid

**Students Who
Applied For Financial Aid:**
63%

Academics

The Lowdown On...
Academics

Degrees Awarded:
Bachelor
Doctorate
Master

Most Popular Majors:
24% Business, Management, and Marketing
16% Liberal Arts
9% Communication and Journalism
8% Education
8% Social Sciences

Undergraduate Schools:
College of Arts and Sciences
College of Social Sciences
Williams College of Business

Student-to-Faculty Ratio:
13:1

Average Course Load:
5 courses (15 credits)

→

Full-Time Faculty:
290

**Faculty with
Terminal Degree:**
83%

Graduation Rates:
Four-Year: 66%
Five-Year: 74%
Six-Year: 75%

Special Degree Options

Combined degree programs – Professional accountancy
program: BSBA accounting, MBA with concentration in
accounting/taxation

Pre-professional programs – Pre-pharmacy, pre-med, pre-law

Minors and miscellaneous programs – Environmental studies,
international studies, jazz, Latin American studies, middle
childhood education, Montessori education, peace studies,
performance studies, women and minorities' studies

AP Test Score Requirements

Possible credit for scores of 3, 4, or 5

IB Test Score Requirements

May be used for credit and/or placement

Academic Clubs

Accounting Society, Advertising Club, Archaeological Society,
Computer Science Club, Entrepreneurial Club, Mermaid
Tavern, Spanish Club

Best Places to Study

Gallagher Student Center, McDonald Library

Did You Know?

Xavier was ranked the **third best all-around college in the Midwestern region** in 2006 by *U.S. News & World Report*, boasting one of the highest retention rates in the nation at 89 percent.

Students Speak Out On...
Academics

{ **"Most teachers are friendly and professional. In the honors program, classes are relatively small."**

Q "Some of the teachers are really cool and interesting people. Other teachers can be pretty dry. I find all of them are **willing to help students** who are looking for assistance and guidance."

Q "The **teachers are approachable**, but too many of them are from Kentucky. The classes are interesting, but not extremely challenging."

Q "There have been a few classes where I thought the professor could have been a little less anal. However, overall, I have found the professors to be **very helpful and extremely interesting**. I am looking forward to getting into my major classes."

Q "For the most part, I really like my teachers. **There are the occasional monotones**, but what school doesn't have those? My classes will be very interesting this semester, and I'm sure very challenging as always."

Q "Pretty much all of the teachers are **very personable and encouraging towards the students**. Although office hours are a minimum requirement by the University, most professors are more than open to meeting a student based on the student's schedule, and they love even those who just stop by to have a casual conversation if nothing else. Often, they will even give out their home phone numbers."

Q "While most professors here do have extended experience in their field, and while the majority of them do an excellent job of teaching, there has been a great migration towards the **use of PowerPoint**, which some students find tougher to learn from."

Q "I personally haven't had any trouble with any of my teachers; some of my friends have, but I think the teachers are great. I find some classes more interesting than others. The **core classes are pretty boring**, but once you get into the higher-level classes, it gets more fun."

Q "Some teachers are very good at conducting their courses, while others are overzealous and try to do too much. I'd say that **two of my six classes are interesting**."

Q "The teachers are personable and generally very interested in the students that they are teaching. The classes are usually quite interesting, because the **teachers here are more concerned with their craft instead of research**."

Q "Obviously, the **teachers vary by department**. Some departments tend to have more laid-back professors, while others have more traditional ones. Even within departments, you can find such differences in professor mentality. Despite these differing approaches, most professors are willing to help out whenever possible. All have office hours, and many will take the time out to help you with any particular problems you may have."

Q "Once you get into the **upper-level courses** of a particular department, the more interesting classes seem to get. Even if the beginning classes in your major don't appeal to you as much as you'd hope, chances are you'll get what you like eventually. Also, you can check in the course catalog and see if what's offered in the next couple of years is interesting to you."

Q "For the most part, I have had very positive experiences with the teachers. Generally, **they are enthusiastic about the subject matter**, more than willing to meet privately to discuss the finer points of the class material, and extremely flexible concerning extraordinary circumstances funerals, appointments, and so on. So far, I have truly enjoyed nearly 75 percent of all the classes I have taken. The required courses sometimes get to be too large and quite elementary, but I sincerely enjoy all the classes I take for my major."

Q "For the most part, the teachers appear dull and non-passionate. This isn't so in every class, though. **You'll find the good teachers** if you look hard enough."

Q "Teachers here at Xavier are **open, friendly, and extremely accommodating**. I was shocked after hearing what friends said about their professors. There are not many TAs (at least that I have witnessed), so you can build a close bond with your teacher. They are truly out to help a student learn and reach his potential, not just dictate a subject to a pack of nameless faces like at larger schools."

Q "In terms of interesting, I guess that really would depend on your bias towards the class or subject before you take it. I mean, if you are an English major and you are forced to take tons of math and science, you may tend to not like the course purely based on the subject, not the class or teacher. That just comes with the territory of a liberal arts education. I would say the majority of the teachers and classes here are very interesting. **Class participation, interesting lectures**, and a general familiarity with the subject and the professor all go towards making a terrific class."

The College Prowler Take On...
Academics

Like any university, the faculty at Xavier is extremely diverse in background, teaching style, and availability. More often than not, the professors avidly encourage students to come during office hours with questions and concerns about course material. Even if you're unlucky enough to catch a bad professor, chances are, they're at least qualified (83 percent of Xavier faculty members hold the highest degrees in their field). Classes are relatively small and have more of a "high school" setting. An average class is about 23 students, which can be helpful in making classes more dynamic and interesting, but if you plan to skip class, chances are the professor is going to notice. The small classes and high level of professor interaction at Xavier are a far cry from the large lectures you'd find at most big universities. If you're looking to nod off amongst a sea of note-takers, it's going to be tough to do well at Xavier.

Xavier has been recognized nationally for many years in the area of academic excellence, and rightly so. With a good balance of introductory courses, as well as seminars and advanced studies available, the University has created a dynamic and challenging environment. The unique ethics/religion and society core ties many of the 100-level courses together so that all students gain a common understanding of their Jesuit education and its ethical implications. The courseload is always challenging enough to keep you busy, but nothing is unmanageable. Ivy League it is not, but based on reputation and results, Xavier is a first-rate academic community.

B

The College Prowler® Grade on
Academics: B

A high Academics grade generally indicates that professors are knowledgeable, accessible, and genuinely interested in their students' welfare. Other determining factors include class size, how well professors communicate, and whether or not classes are engaging.

Local Atmosphere

The Lowdown On...
Local Atmosphere

Region:
Midwest

City, State:
Cincinnati, OH

Setting:
Medium-sized city

Distance from Chicago:
5 hours

Distance from Cleveland:
4 hours

Points of Interest:
B.B. Riverboats
Cincinnati Art Museum
Cincinnati Zoo and Botanical Garden
Eden Park
Great American Ballpark
Newport Aquarium and IMAX Theater
Paul Brown Stadium

Closest Shopping Malls:

Rookwood Commons and Pavilion

2699 Edmondson Road
Cincinnati

(513) 241-5800

www.shoprookwood.com

Tri-County Mall

11700 Princeton Pike
Cincinnati

On the corner of Princeton Pike and Kemper Road

(513) 346-4482

www.tricountymall.com

Closest Movie Theaters:

AMC Newport on The Levee 20

I-471 at Exit 5
Newport, KY

(859) 261-8100

(Closest Movie Theaters, continued)

Esquire Theater

320 Ludlow Avenue
Cincinnati

(513) 281-8750

Kenwood Towne Center

7875 Montgomery Road
Cincinnati

(513) 699-1500

Showcase Cinemas Cincinnati

1701 Showcase Drive
Cincinnati

(513) 699-1500

Major Sports Teams:

Cincinnati Reds (baseball)
Cincinnati Bengals (football)
Cincinnati Mighty Ducks (minor league hockey)

City Web Sites

www.cincinnati.com

www.cincyusa.com

www.cincy.com

Did You Know?

5 Fun Facts about Cincinnati:

- Used to be known as "Porkopolis," due to the **staggering pig population**.
- Home of the **first professional baseball team**, the Cincinnati Red Stockings (1869).
- Home of one of the United States' **first municipal police forces**.
- The city was **originally called Fort Washington**, but the name was changed in 1802.
- *Traffic*, *Rain Man*, and *Eight Men Out* were all **filmed in Cincinnati**.

Famous People from Cincinnati:

George Clooney (Actor, over-the-hill heartthrob)

Carmen Electra (Sex goddess, actress)

Charles Manson (Serial killer)

Sarah Jessica Parker (Actress, sex symbol)

Pete Rose (Would-be baseball hall-of-famer)

Harriet Beecher Stowe (American Civil War author)

Steven Spielberg (Movie producer, billionaire)

William Howard Taft (The fattest U.S. president ever)

Ted Turner (Tycoon, president of TNT and TBS)

Local Slang:

Coney – A small hot dog covered in Cincinnati chili and shredded cheese

Please? – What a Cincinnatian will say instead of "Excuse me?" or "Pardon?"

Pop – Soda, soft drink

Sucker – A lollipop

Students Speak Out On...
Local Atmosphere

> "It's a mix of urban ghetto and rich, white, suburban kids. Keep off the streets at night, and go to parties with a group of people. It's the best way to stay safe."

Q "Cincinnati is mostly a boring, conservative, Midwestern city. However, **it is a particularly large city**, and there are things to do."

Q "I would recommend checking out the Cincinnati Art Museum. It is small, but it has a **cool antiquities section**. Be careful, though, 'you break, you buy!'"

Q "It's, **in one word, conservative**. There are a number of other universities. Stay away from Over-the-Rhine (or so I've heard), and there are quite a few things to visit."

Q "Cincinnati has a lot to do. For sports teams, you've got the Reds and Bengals. I'd **stay out of Norwood** because any party of about three people or more will get broken up."

Q "The town I am currently in is pretty wild. There is always plenty to do on the weekends and everyone enjoys having fun. The **University of Cincinnati is here**, but nobody likes them. Stuff to stay away from during the first semester is going out too much during the week if you're a freshman. Get your priorities straight!"

Q "I have visited friends who go to Miami of Ohio and UC. I tend to stay on campus, but I have been to **Reds and Bengals games**, as well as a couple of concerts. Check out Kings Island, it's awesome."

Q "The campus is set in a suburban environment. The atmosphere is **no more than a couple of local bars**, which act as college hangouts. University of Cincinnati is located about 15 minutes away. UC is closer to the heart of the city. Some parts of the neighborhood can be rough, so be cautious. However, this never keeps students from walking around at night."

Q "At Xavier, there is a clear division between people in the surrounding towns. I would say there is **some sense of resentment towards the students** and the institution of Xavier University by some citizens of Norwood, but for the most part, it is a great place to live. The University of Cincinnati is literally 15 minutes away. That makes rivalry games huge around here. Miami of Ohio is also considerably close to Xavier. As with any urban setting, there are definitely spots of Cincinnati you may want to avoid or be careful around. For the most part, however, Cincinnati is a great place to live and visit."

Q "The atmosphere in this town sucks pretty bad. There **isn't really a whole lot to do, unless you want to spend some serious cash**. There are other universities in the area, which makes the scene a little better simply due to the availability of many, many parties. I'd say that it would be wise to stay away from certain parts of the downtown area, as they're extremely dangerous. The Playhouse in Eden Park, the Cincinnati Art Museum, and a football game in the Pit at Elder High School are certainly things every person should try at least once in his or her life."

Q "Cincinnati has the characteristics common of any middle U.S. city. There are professional sports teams to watch, movies to go to, places to hang out, and so on. **Just across the bridge is the Newport Aquarium**, an interesting place, though not cheap. The only other big university in the city is the University of Cincinnati, but the Universities of Dayton and Miami of Ohio are only an hour away. These are places where students frequently visit."

The College Prowler Take On...
Local Atmosphere

Cincinnati is a very interesting city to live in, especially if you're not originally from here. The atmosphere of "the Nati," as it's called by many of its locals, is culturally diverse, but very conservative. There are different pockets of culture scattered throughout the area, with strong German influences in almost all of the architecture. The University of Cincinnati is the only other major college in the area, and it serves as Xavier's rival in just about everything. Some of the must-see attractions include the brand new Great American Ballpark, home of the Cincinnati Reds, the Cincinnati Zoo, and the Newport Aquarium, which is just across the river in Kentucky. While there is a multitude of places to explore in the Cincinnati area, there are a couple spots wandering students should probably avoid. Over-the-Rhine, a struggling neighborhood that suffers from drug infestation, crime, and negligent landlords is a place you don't want to be after dark.

Cincinnati is a unique place to live and go to school. Many students who come from other areas are often amazed at how different the city can be from their home towns, for better or worse. However, Cincinnati is not all that it could be, as far as safety downtown, cultural events, and things to do in general. While you won't go out of your mind from boredom, don't confuse "the Nati" with Chicago, New York, or Los Angeles.

The College Prowler® Grade on

Local Atmosphere: C+

A high Local Atmosphere grade indicates that the area surrounding campus is safe and scenic. Other factors include nearby attractions, proximity to other schools, and the town's attitude toward students.

Safety & Security

The Lowdown On...
Safety & Security

Number of XU Police:
30 officers

Police Phone:
(513) 745-1000

Safety Services:
24-hour foot, bike, and vehicle patrols

Campus shuttle

Emergency phones

Rape defense classes (RAD)

Health Services:
Allergy injections and vaccinations

Direct nursing care

Nutrition Center

Support, counseling, and information about disease prevention

→

Health Center Phone:

McGrath Health and
Counseling Center

1714 Cleneay Ave.
(next to the Cohen Lot)

(513) 745-3022

health@xavier.edu

Health Center Office Hours:

Nurse hours (walk-in):
Monday–Friday
8:30 a.m.–4:30 p.m.

Physician hours (walk-in):
Monday 12:30 p.m.–3 p.m.,
Tuesday 10 a.m.–12 p.m.,
Wednesday 10 a.m.–12 p.m.
and 3 p.m.–4:30 p.m.,
Thursday 2 p.m.–4:30 p.m.,
Friday 10 a.m.–12 p.m.
and 2:30 p.m.–4:30 p.m.

Did You Know?

Campus police sit in their cars with the lights off at night in the parking lots to keep watch. There were **problems of break-ins in the past**, but the police force has been extra vigilant as of late. You can read about all their busts every week in the campus newspaper, the *Newswire*, which has a section devoted to humorous and interesting police notes.

Students Speak Out On...
Safety & Security

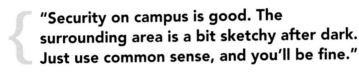

> **"Security on campus is good. The surrounding area is a bit sketchy after dark. Just use common sense, and you'll be fine."**

Q "Security is tight on campus. **There was a problem with cars getting broken into** and bums getting into dorms. The funny thing is that some of the hobos are probably cleaner than my roommate!"

Q "**On-campus security is very safe**, although sometimes unfriendly. I wouldn't wander too far off campus alone, though."

Q "I find on-campus security to be quite adequate. Security officers are abundant, and they are **always available if you need some sort of help**."

Q "Campus police at Xavier are great. **They're very reasonable when it comes to discipline**, and they make the campus a very safe place. Campus is also pretty well lit the entire year."

Q "Anywhere on campus, I would feel safe at almost anytime, particularly when I'm with other people. Campus police are not far from anywhere, **there are emergency phones in various places**, and everywhere is pretty well lit. There is no denying that off campus can be unsafe in certain places at certain times, but avoiding going out late at night or alone leaves little to worry about. There is a useful shuttle service that operates a good portion of the day and night, as well, making night ventures safe and easy."

Q "Xavier has a small police force directly across the street from campus. They patrol all the time. You can tell they are out to protect and keep the school safe. Also, if the Cincinnati police or fire department is ever needed, they are close enough to respond in a hurry. Plus, the fact that **Xavier is a close-knit place** makes it all the more reassuring when it comes to safety. If you see someone you don't know, or see someone doing something shady, he or she will be reported right away. Even in the dorms, you can't get in without a key or being with someone who lives in the dorm."

Q "I have **never heard of any on-campus attacks** upon students. There is an Xavier University police force, and they are always on call. There is also a shuttle which will take students to locations as far as a mile off campus. This is especially useful during late nights at school. I believe they're available for parties, as well."

Q "I've never been worried about the security here at Xavier. **I always see campus police driving around**."

Q "**This place is a total bubble**. There are absolutely no security issues when you live on campus."

The College Prowler Take On...
Safety & Security

Campus safety is a high priority for the administration at Xavier, and it shows. Campus police vehicles are on frequent patrol 24 hours a day, and everywhere on campus is well lit, so one can take a midnight stroll without being accosted (unless you're into that sort of thing). The University has in place emergency call-boxes throughout the campus, so that if there ever was any trouble, the campus police are able to respond fairly quickly. As long as you are on Xavier University property, you feel relatively safe. While neighboring streets are not quite as pristine, there seems to be a heavily-enforced bubble that keeps those who live and work at Xavier safe.

The campus police do everything within their means to make sure that everyone on campus can live, work, study, and play in a safe environment. Unfortunately, with crime problems in the surrounding communities, especially Norwood, there is only so much the University can do. On campus is one of the safest places in the county you can be, but unfortunately, the same cannot be said for the streets outside of Xavier, where many students live in apartments and houses.

The College Prowler® Grade on

Safety & Security: B

A high grade in Safety & Security means that students generally feel safe, campus police are visible, blue-light phones and escort services are readily available, and safety precautions are not overly necessary.

Computers

The Lowdown On...
Computers

High-Speed Network?
Yes

Number of Labs:
720

Wireless Network?
Yes

Number of Computers:
225

Operating Systems:

Mac OS, Windows

Free Software:

None

24-Hour Labs:

Yes, computer lab in Gallagher Student Center

Charge to Print?

Varies, most labs have no charge. Some charge 10 cents per color page.

Did You Know?

Every user on campus is now integrated into a MyXu e-mail system that replaced the old system in 2004. Campus e-mail is now Web-based, so you can access your account at any computer with Internet access. With this addition, **many professors are gearing their lectures toward the Blackboard online classroom system** and even posting their entire PowerPoint lectures online.

Students Speak Out On...
Computers

{ **"The network at Xavier is fast enough. However, I would bring a computer if I were you."**

 "I would recommend bringing a computer simply for convenience; **you will definitely use it a lot.**"

"Just about everyone has their own PC, so it's best to have one yourself. However, **you can survive just using the labs.**"

"The network can be a pain if it's not properly set up. Labs are, of course, in use, but **there are certain times of the day when you can find free space.** Plus, you can always go to the lab in the psychology building. Having your own computer greatly depends on how often you use it."

"I didn't have a computer my freshman year, and I wish I had. I think it is best to have one, but **a printer isn't always necessary**, because there is free printing in the labs."

"There are problems on the network on a few occasions, as with any network, but **generally, it works well and is easy to get hooked up to.** There are various computer labs around, which usually aren't full, except during certain weeks such as finals week. Computers in the labs admittedly don't always work right, but lab staff is usually helpful."

Q "Most people do have their own computers, because there is **Internet access for two people in the rooms**. However, it is not a big deal if you don't have a computer. There are plenty of labs on our campus."

Q "The computer **labs are always crowded**, and it's nearly impossible to run in their just to print something, because you'll be waiting behind about 20 other idiots. I would highly suggest bringing your own computer, especially a laptop, since it can be hard to get work done in a dorm room. Also, it's nice to be able to bring a laptop to the library and write a paper in peace and quiet."

Q "The network is very fast. The **dorms at Xavier run on a T-1 connection**, so speeds can be as high as 1 MB/sec. There are restrictors on certain entertainment Web sites, as well as file-sharing programs (Kazaa, for example), however, educational sites are given high priority, and downloads are very fast. The labs are not usually crowded, and they are located sparingly throughout the campus in different buildings and in every dorm. Every student should bring a personal computer, for at least communication and entertainment reasons. However, the lab computers offer word-processing and standard school programs (Adobe, Excel) if a student does not have a computer."

Q "The computer labs always have a spot or two open for those people needing to print out a last minute paper, or send a life or death e-mail to mom and dad. There are **several labs, the library, and a 24-hour lab**. Also, tons of people have them in their dorms, so you can get by without one. You don't have to bring a computer."

Q "The **labs are usually crowded**, but not so crowded that you can't find an open computer. It would certainly be wise to bring a computer with you, since the labs are only open certain hours of the day. It's just a better situation to have your own computer in your room for those emergencies that tend to creep up around deadline time."

Q "I highly **recommend bringing your own computer** for the simple convenience. Classes often take up space in the computer labs at the library."

The College Prowler Take On...
Computers

For dorm users, the computer network is fast, and setting it up with your system is relatively painless. Occasionally, there will be some down time due to technical problems, but overall, everyone in the dorms has a reliable Internet connection. However, don't expect to go on a downloading rampage! The University has bandwidth restrictions in place on file sharing programs such as Kazaa and Morpheus. With everyone having a high-speed connection in their dorm room, it is not uncommon to see a group of Xavier students huddled around an X-Box 360, battling it out against their friends across campus in games like "Halo" and "Madden '06." There are enough computer labs that getting to a computer is never a problem, but most students bring their own computers or laptops. The Gallagher Student Center lends out laptops for students to use on an hourly basis at no charge, but the laptops are notoriously low on batteries, sometimes making them more of a headache than they're worth.

Xavier has a good ratio of computers to students, making it easy on those who choose not to bring their own computer to campus. The network is adequate enough to serve the needs of its users, usually without too many problems such as viruses. There has been an effort on the University's part to make the laptop system in the Gallagher Center more conducive to everyday use, but the students could use more than just one lab operating 24 hours. Other than that, most Musketeers are happily plugged in at Xavier.

B+

The College Prowler® Grade on
Computers: B+

A high grade in Computers designates that computer labs are available, the computer network is easily accessible, and the campus' computing technology is up-to-date.

Facilities

The Lowdown On...
Facilities

Student Center:
Gallagher Student Center

Athletic Center:
O'Connor Sports Center

Libraries:
2

Popular Places to Chill:
Lounge areas in Gallagher
Residential Mall
Ryan's Pub
Victory Perk

Campus Size:
125 acres

What Is There to Do on Campus?

During the day, the Gallagher Student Center is the place to be. Whether you need to study, catch the 12 p.m. *SportsCenter*, shoot some pool, or just get a cup of coffee, the "G-Spot" is where it's at. At night, you can catch a movie or a play in the brand new theater within the student center, as well. While some students enjoy the relaxed atmosphere of Gallagher, others prefer to head down to the O'Connor Sports Center to pump some iron, take a swim, or play hoops.

Movie Theater on Campus?

No. However, movies are shown in the Gallagher Center's auditorium from time to time.

Bowling on Campus?

No.

Bar on Campus?

Yes, there is Ryan's Pub in the Gallagher Student Center.

Coffeehouse on Campus?

Yes, there is Victory Perk in the Gallagher Student Center.

Favorite Things to Do

Aside from all the day-to-day amenities of the Gallagher Center, there is often karaoke or live music of some kind in Ryan's Pub, located on the ground floor. Ryan's will also be packed for football games and before and after home basketball games. Many students also like to attend evening jazzercise and aerobics classes at O'Connor. Other students just like to hang out on the Residential Mall, in front of the dorms, and play Frisbee.

Students Speak Out On...
Facilities

{ **"The student center and the basketball arena are both gorgeous. However, there aren't a lot of activities in the student center, mostly just offices. The athletic center also needs to be replaced."**

Q "The student center is poorly named, because there is little there for students. The Cintas Center arena is great, but **O'Connor is lacking.**"

Q "Everything is nice on campus, except for the construction. **Xavier prides itself on its facilities,** and it's obvious."

Q "**O'Connor is a very nice facility to work out in.** There are racquetball and basketball courts, along with a variety of free weights, treadmills, stairmasters, and more."

Q "The **facilities at Xavier are beautiful.** They are the best I have ever seen."

Q "**The sports center, where the regular students get to work out, is below average**, but trying to improve. There aren't a whole lot of fitness machines, but the hours are really good. The student center is shiny and new, but not really good for much else other than getting an overpriced sub or the occasional cup of coffee. They change the hours that they are open all the time, so you never know when you can actually eat there."

Q "The athletic facilities are **a little bit of a walk from the dorms**, however, they are more than sufficient for weightlifting (free weights and pulley weights) and cardio (treadmills, stair-climbers, elliptical machines). There are also six basketball courts located at the O'Connor Sports Center, along with three racquetball courts. The student center, which was criticized in its first year for not being student-oriented is now living up to its name by offering free video games, relatively late-closing restaurants, laptop and board game check-outs (free with student ID), and frequent movies or performances in the theater on the bottom floor."

Q "The student center is at the center of campus. **Playing games, watching TV, grabbing a burger, or just having a cup of coffee** are some of the possibilities and reasons to attend the Gallagher Center. O'Conner Sports Complex is perfect for sports fans. It has a pool, a weight room, racquetball courts, basketball courts, and aerobics on most nights. Cintas Center is new and beautiful for student dining or basketball/volleyball games. Computer labs tend to have 'issues' at times, but someone is always there to fix something if you need it."

Q "The facilities are very nice. They are all kept clean, and we usually have **all the latest equipment available**. The Gallagher Student Center is certainly among the best in the nation as far as amenities for the students, events, and things to do on a study break."

Q "The facilities at the sports center are decent at best. They could really be updated, or even rebuilt, if the necessary funds were raised for it. The computers now have flat screens in the library, so they are pretty nice. The **student center is relatively new**, so that is about as nice as it comes."

The College Prowler Take On...
Facilities

For the most part, the facilities on campus at Xavier are first class. The O'Connor Sports Center is a popular place for students to work out, and it also includes an extensive gym and weight room. The OSC also houses an Olympic-sized swimming pool, three basketball courts, and holds aerobics classes regularly. There are many computer labs in the academic buildings and in each dorm, so students have access to computers 24 hours a day. Most of the equipment is new and is networked across the entire campus.

The Gallagher Student Center functions as the centerpiece for the campus. A variety of shops and restaurants, including Starbucks and Burger King, as well as tables, sofas, and flat-screen TVs make the student center a popular place for students to relax and study during the day. The student center also houses a performing arts stage and seating bowl. Unfortunately, upon it's opening, many of the University's offices were moved into the four-level structure, so it doesn't truly feel like it belongs to the students. This explains the student resentment in some of the quotes.

B+

The College Prowler® Grade on
Facilities: B+

A high Facilities grade indicates that the campus is aesthetically pleasing and well-maintained; facilities are state-of-the-art, and libraries are exceptional. Other determining factors include the quality of both athletic and student centers and an abundance of things to do on campus.

Campus Dining

The Lowdown On...
Campus Dining

Freshman Meal Plan Requirement?

Yes

Meal Plan Average Cost:

$1,765 per semester

($655 per semester for commuters)

Places to Grab a Bite with Your Meal Plan:

Burger King

Food: Burgers and fries, breakfast sandwiches

Location: Ground level, Gallagher Student Center

Hours: Monday–Thursday 11 a.m.–7 p.m., Friday 11 a.m.–3:30 p.m.

Iggy's Pizza

Food: Made-to-order subs, sandwiches, and bagels

Location: Ground level, Gallagher Student Center

Hours: Monday–Thursday 11 a.m.–7 p.m., Friday 11 a.m.–3:30 p.m.

James E. Hoff Dining Hall (the Caf)

Food: Buffet-style, all-you-care-to-eat, rotating menu

Location: Lower level, Cintas Center

Hours: Monday–Friday 7:30 a.m.–10:15 a.m., 11 a.m.–2:30 p.m., 4:30 p.m.–7:30 p.m., Saturday–Sunday 11 a.m.–2:30 p.m., 4:30 p.m.–7:30 p.m.

Ryan's Pub

Food: Sandwiches, salads, appetizers, draft beer

Location: Ground level, Gallagher Student Center

Hours: Monday–Friday 11:30 a.m.–2 p.m., 4:30 p.m.–10:30 p.m., Saturday 4:30 p.m.–10:30 p.m., Sunday 4:30 p.m.–10:30 p.m.

Subway

Food: Subs, cookies

Location: Ground level, Gallagher Student Center

Hours: Monday–Thursday 8 a.m.–1 a.m., Friday–Saturday 8 a.m.– 2 a.m., Sunday 11 a.m.–1 a.m.

Victory Perk

Food: Coffee and pastries

Location: First floor, Gallagher Student Center

Hours: Monday–Thursday 7:30 a.m.–11:30 a.m., 3 p.m.–7 p.m., Friday 7:30 a.m.–11:30 a.m.

Off-Campus Places to Use Your Meal Plan:

None

24-Hour On-Campus Eating?

No

Student Favorites:

Burger King

Iggy's Pizza

James E. Hoff Dining Hall

Other Options

Students sometimes don't find what they're looking for in the Caf (Hoff Dining Hall) or in Gallagher, but luckily a multitude of pizza and Chinese places will deliver right to the dorms until as late as 2 a.m. on weekends. And you wonder where the Freshman 15 comes from.

Did You Know?

The **dining hall is equipped with many overhead TVs to watch football**, game shows, or just to fill the awkward silences during mealtime conversations. Unlimited food, TV, and hanging out with your friends? It's a wonder anyone ever leaves.

Students Speak Out On...
Campus Dining

{ **"The dining hall and the overall quality of food are pretty decent when compared to other schools."**

Q "There are a decent amount of choices, but the food here is **overpriced and lacking in originality**."

Q "The food at Xavier is edible. Actually, it's good, but it **does get old quickly**. Pretty much everyone can be found in the Caf or at the G-Spot eating."

Q "Personally, I like the food at the cafeteria in the Cintas Center. A lot of my friends say they don't, but **I think it's pretty good**. If you ask me, a good turkey sandwich with some honey mustard sauce will go a long way."

Q "The **best spots to dine are definitely not on campus**."

Q "Iggy's is a good place to eat. **The dining halls are okay during the week**, but stink on the weekend nights. I would give the total food package a 'C.'"

Q "I like going to the 'Caf' or dining hall. Not only is the food great, but it's a great place to hang out. A lot of the times, **we just hang out after we have eaten, and you will see all your friends**. There is also Iggy's Pizza and Burger King in Gallagher."

Q "The **food served on campus at Xavier is hit-or-miss**. Sometimes, the Caf will serve a really good dinner, other times, everything looks like vomit. I've heard it's much better than other schools, but it's certainly not your mom's home cooking. The best part is that no matter what, you can always get cereal (Lucky Charms, Cinnamon Toast Crunch, Cocoa Pebbles, and so on). Soft-serve ice cream is also a delicacy at the X. If you want to pretend you're eating at a restaurant and still be able to use your meal plan, then go to Ryan's Pub. The service is usually pretty slow, but the food is pretty good."

Q "The food at the Hoff Dining Center (the Caf) is rather good, **offering healthy food along with college staples such as pizza**, hamburgers, and lunch meats. The Gallagher Student Center offers a wide variety of food. There is a deli, an ice cream stand, a Burger King, and the pub, which offers different American foods."

Q "The dining hall in Cintas Center is pretty good, actually. There is a wide variety on the menu every night. Sometimes simple, sometimes exotic. No matter what, there are your **classic cheeseburgers (veggie and hamburgers also available), fries, and a salad bar** every night. There is a Burger King or Iggy's Pizza to go along with Ryan's Pub, all on campus."

The College Prowler Take On...
Campus Dining

The school's basketball arena, the Cintas Center, also plays host to the James E. Hoff Student Dining Hall. This dining hall serves as the primary source for meals on a day-to-day basis. Commonly referred to as "the Caf," the Hoff Dining Hall is the money spot for a good breakfast after an all-night cram session. Lunch and dinner are usually decent, but the cafeteria can come up with some weird selections. Students often complain that the dining hall isn't open past 7:30 p.m. To remedy this problem, there are a variety of late-night food outlets in the Gallagher Student Center, with most of the restaurants being open until 11 p.m. Burger King seems to be the most popular of these selections, along with Iggy's Pizza, which serves subs, sandwiches, and bagels made to order.

Overall, the food selection at Xavier is decent, but can sometimes be scarce, due to there being only two dining locations. Luckily for the students, *http://xudining.com* will tell you if there's nothing exiting on the menu, from the comfort of your own dorm. If that's the case, calling in a pizza delivery is the popular choice at XU. With the lack of choices and no 24-hour eateries to be found on campus, Xavier's dining situation definitely has room for improvement.

C+

The College Prowler® Grade on

Campus Dining: C+

Our grade on Campus Dining addresses the quality of both school-owned dining halls and independent on-campus restaurants as well as the price, availability, and variety of food.

Off-Campus Dining

The Lowdown On...
Off-Campus Dining

Restaurant Prowler:
Popular Places to Eat

Bonefish Grill

Food: Seafood

2737 Madison Road
Hyde Park

(513) 321-5222

Price: $8–$15 per person

Hours: Monday–Thursday
5 p.m.–10 p.m.,
Friday 5 p.m.–11 p.m.,
Saturday 4 p.m.–11 p.m.,
Sunday 4 p.m.–9 p.m.

Buca Di Beppo

Food: Italian

2635 Edmondson Road
Rookwood Commons
and Pavilion

(513) 396-7673

Price: $7–$12 per person
(family style)

Hours: Monday–Thursday
5 p.m.–10 p.m.,
Friday 5 p.m.–11 p.m.,
Saturday 12 p.m.–11 p.m.,
Sunday 12 p.m.–10 p.m.

Buffalo Wild Wings

Food: Wings

2692 Madison Road
Suite A7

(513) 351-9464

Price: $8–$15 per person

Hours: Monday–Thursday
11 a.m.–1 a.m.,
Friday–Saturday
11 a.m.–2 a.m.,
Sunday 11 a.m.–12 a.m.

Chipotle Mexican Grill

Food: Mexican

3725 Paxton Avenue
Hyde Park

(513) 631-3800

Price: $5–$8 per person

Hours: Monday–Sunday
11 a.m.–10 p.m.

Don Pablo's

Food: Mexican

2962 Madison Road Suite 1
Rookwood Commons
and Pavilion

(513) 631-1356

Price: $8–$15 per person

Hours: Monday–Thursday
11 a.m.–10 p.m., Friday–
Saturday 11 a.m.–11 p.m.,
Sunday 11 a.m.–10 p.m.

First Watch

Food: Breakfast, lunch

2692 Madison Road
Suite N3, Rookwood
Commons and Pavilion

(513) 531-7430

Price: $6–$10 per person

Hours: Monday–Sunday
7 a.m.–2:30 p.m.

Graeter's

Food: Ice cream

2704 Erie Avenue
Hyde Park

(513) 321-6221

Price: $2–$5 per person

Hours: Monday–Sunday
9 a.m.–10:45 p.m.

J. Alexander's

Food: Upscale American,
burgers

2629 Edmondson Road
Rookwood Commons and
Pavilion

(513) 531-7495

Price: $10–$15 per person

Hours: Monday–Thursday
11 a.m.–11 a.m.,
Friday–Saturday
11 a.m.–12 a.m.,
Sunday 11 a.m.–10 p.m.

LaRosa's Pizzeria

Food: Pizza, Italian

4702 Montgomery Road
Norwood

(513) 351-2316

Price: $8–$12 per person

Hours: Monday–Thursday
11 a.m.–10 p.m.,
Friday–Saturday
11 a.m.–11:30 p.m.,
Sunday 12 p.m.–10 p.m.

Max and Erma's

Food: Family, American

2631 Edmondson Road
Rookwood Commons

(513) 631-7888

Price: $6–$15 per person

Hours: Monday–Thursday
11 a.m.–10:30 p.m.,
Friday–Saturday
11 a.m.–11:30 p.m.,
Sunday 11 a.m.–10 p.m.

Montgomery Inn-Ribs King

Food: Ribs, steaks,
sandwiches

9440 Montgomery Road
Northeast

(513) 791-3482

Price: $10–$25 per person

Hours: Sunday 3 p.m.–
9:30 p.m., Monday–Thursday
11 a.m.–11 p.m., Friday–
Saturday 3 p.m.–12 p.m.

PF Chang's China Bistro

Food: Chinese

2633 Edmondson Road
Rookwood Commons
and Pavilion

(513) 631-4567

Price: $10–$15 per person

Hours: Sunday–Thursday
11 a.m.–11 p.m.,
Friday–Saturday 11 a.m.–
12 a.m.

Skyline Chili

Food: Chili

3081 Madison Road
Hyde Park

(513) 871-2930

Price: $2–$5 per person

Hours: Monday–Thursday
10:30 a.m.–11 p.m.,
Friday–Saturday 10:30 a.m.–
2:30 a.m., Sunday 11 a.m.–
10 p.m.

Steak 'n Shake

Food: Steakburgers, desserts

9770 Montgomery Road
Cincinnati

(513) 984-1202

Price: $4–$8 per person

Hours: Daily 24 hours

Waffle House
Food: Breakfast
2391 E. Sharon Road
(513) 771-5099
Price: $3–$7 per person
Hours: Daily 24 hours

Zip's Cafe
Food: Burgers
1036 Delta Avenue
(513) 871-9876
Price: $3–$7 per person
Hours: Sunday–Thursday
10:30 a.m.–10:30 p.m.,
Friday–Saturday
10:30 a.m.–11:30 p.m.

Student Favorites:
Buffalo Wild Wings
Skyline Chili

24-Hour Eating:
Steak 'n Shake
Waffle House

Closest Grocery Stores:
The Kroger Co. (24 hours)
3760 Paxton Avenue
Hyde Park
(513) 871-4142

Other Places to Check Out:
Indigo's (Italian)
Jerusalem Café
Papa John's
TGI Fridays)
Wendy's

Best Pizza:
LaRosa's Pizzeria

Best Chinese:
P.F. Chang's China Bistro

Best Breakfast:
First Watch

Best Wings:
Buffalo Wild Wings

Best Healthy:
First Watch

Best Place to Take Your Parents:
Montgomery Inn-Ribs King

Students Speak Out On...
Off-Campus Dining

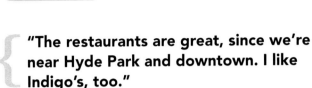

"The restaurants are great, since we're near Hyde Park and downtown. I like Indigo's, too."

Q "Buca di Beppo's is good, and the **Jerusalem Café is a must see**."

Q "If you like Cincinnati chili, then the food is good, but there is **no good authentic Italian food** around."

Q "The restaurants off campus are good. There is Zip's, Montgomery Inn, and several others. You always have the **option of going cheap or expensive**."

Q "Chipotle is located over near the Hyde Park Kroger. There are tons of fast food places up Montgomery Road, including a **Wendy's for all those late-night munchies**."

Q "There are a number of good and bad places off campus, like in any town. Everyone talks about **the local specialty, Montgomery Inn ribs**, which I have never had, but will try one day. There are also restaurants from pretty much every national chain somewhere nearby."

Q "The **restaurants off campus are great**. There are plenty of them in Rookwood, Hyde Park, and Newport, Kentucky. These include TGI Fridays, Bonefish Grill, J. Alexander's, and PF Chang's."

Q "There is always **Papa John's**, as well as the other major chains."

Q "There are several Chinese restaurants that **all deliver late into the night**. There are fast food spots all around the city surrounding Xavier. PF Chang's, J. Alexander's, and Montgomery Inn are also very close."

Q "If you want to eat off campus, you have to have a car. There are **a ton of chain restaurants** right up 71 (PF Chang's, Buca, Max & Erma's, Chipotle). If you want to go to a cooler place, try Hyde Park Square or Mt. Adams."

Q "There are a couple of good places to eat off campus. One lesser known favorite is Zip's Café, which is located in Mt. Lookout. It offers burgers and fries for a very affordable price. Cincinnati chili restaurants like Skyline are located everywhere. **Exceptional ice cream can be found in nearby Hyde Park at Graeter's**. More expensive restaurants include spots like Montgomery Inn, which offers fantastic barbeque at prices that might be out of range for most students. However, during parent's weekend, this is a nice place to visit."

The College Prowler Take On...
Off-Campus Dining

On the weekends, or on special occasions, Xavier students tend to flock toward the trendy restaurants in neighboring areas. Rookwood, an upscale shopping center, is home to many of the dining choices that XU students frequent on a regular basis. Buffalo Wild Wings, PF Chang's, First Watch, and Buca di Beppo are just a few of the dining options in Rookwood that are extremely popular at Xavier. Those preferring a different atmosphere often venture to Hyde Park, where cozy restaurants like Zip's Café and Graeter's ice cream offer a more authentic Cincinnati feel. Hyde Park can be a little pricier, but there are tons of great places to choose from. Any time you mention food and Cincinnati in the same sentence, you're obligated to at least make reference to Skyline Chili, the city's trademark dish. The special brand of chili served with spaghetti, cheese, or hot dogs is a favorite among locals. For out-of-towners, it may take some getting used to, but you can't experience Cincinnati without at least trying the stuff. (Don't forget the Tums.)

The off-campus dining experience at Xavier is convenient and full of a wide array of choices. Whatever you're in the mood for, there is sure to be a place within a few miles to fill your stomach at a reasonable price. The best part about it is most of the popular restaurants are all clumped together in Rookwood and Hyde Park, so you don't even have to decide what you're in the mood for until you get where you're going. Whether you develop a taste for Skyline Chili or not, there are still plenty of great places to feed your face off campus.

A-

The College Prowler® Grade on
Off-Campus
Dining: A-

A high Off-Campus Dining grade implies that off-campus restaurants are affordable, accessible, and worth visiting. Other factors include the variety of cuisine and the availability of alternative options (vegetarian, vegan, Kosher, etc.).

Campus Housing

The Lowdown On...
Campus Housing

Room Types:
Brockman Hall offers double and triple occupancy dormitories, while Buenger, Husman, and Kuhlman halls have double-, triple-, and quadruple-occupancy suite-style living. Apartment-style living is also available for upperclassmen.

Best Dorms:
Buenger Hall
Commons Apartments
Kuhlman Hall

Worst Dorm:
Brockman Hall

Undergrads Living on Campus:
48%

Number of Dormitories:
9

Number of University-Owned Apartments:
6

→

Residence Halls:

1019 Dana Apartments

Floors: 3

Total Occupancy: 8

Bathrooms: Community
(1 per unit)

Coed: Yes

Residents: Juniors, seniors

Room Types: Single-
occupancy efficiency
apartments

Special Features: Laundry,
mail, furnishings, utilities
included.

Brockman Hall

Floors: 4

Total Occupancy: 257

Bathrooms: Community
(shared by wing)

Coed: Yes

Residents: Freshmen

Room Types: Double- and
triple-occupancy rooms

Special Features: Only
all first-year dorm, laundry,
full kitchen, vending,
recreational room, first floor
is substance free.

Buenger Hall

Floors: 4

Total Occupancy: 205

Bathrooms: Private
(1 ½ per suite)

Coed: Yes

Residents: Freshmen honor
students only

Room Types: Double-,
triple-, and quadruple-
occupancy suites

Special Features: Basement
lounge, vending, study
lounges, full kitchen, laundry,
music room.

Commons Apartments

Floors: 4

Total Occupancy: 274

Bathrooms: Private
(2 per apartment)

Coed: Yes

Residents: Upperclassmen

Room Types: Two-, three- and
four-bedroom apartments

Special Features: Spacious
lounges, kitchen in every
apartment, vending, laundry,
dining and common areas.

Husman Hall

Floors: 4

Total Occupancy: 289

Bathrooms: Private
(1 per every 2 rooms)

Coed: Yes

(Husman Hall, continued)

Residents: Freshmen, sophomores

Room Types: Double- and triple-occupancy suites

Special Features: Laundry, lounges, recreational room, fourth floor permits smoking.

Kuhlman Hall

Floors: 6

Total Occupancy: 450

Bathrooms: Private (1 per every 2 rooms)

Coed: Yes

Residents: Freshmen, sophomores

Room Types: Double-occupancy suites

Special Features: Fifth floor is substance free, laundry, vending, full kitchen, study lounges, recreation rooms.

Manor House Apartments

Floors: 2

Total Occupancy: 24

Bathrooms: Private

Coed: Yes

Residents: Upperclassmen

Room Types: Double- and single-occupancy apartments

Special Features: For substance-free sophomores, men's basketball players, juniors, seniors, and graduate students, laundry, mail.

Village Apartments

Floors: 3

Total Occupancy: 224

Bathrooms: Private (1 per unit, 2 in 4-bedroom apartments)

Coed: Yes

Residents: Upperclassmen

Room Types: Townhouse apartments, two-bedroom flats, four-bedroom apartments

Special Features: Laundry, vending, multipurpose room, mail room.

University Apartments

Floors: 3

Total Occupancy: 24

Bathrooms: Private

Coed: Yes

Residents: Juniors, seniors

Room Types: Twelve one-bedroom apartments, double occupancy

Special Features: Completely substance-free, laundry, mail.

Housing Offered:

Singles: 3%

Doubles: 60%

Triples/Suites: 3%

Apartments: 33%

Other: 1%

Bed Type

80"x 36", or 72"x 36", extra-long sheets recommended

Cleaning Service?

Yes, every residence hall cleaned weekly by a cleaning staff

What You Get

Bed, closet, desk, cable and Internet access, microwave and refrigerator (Buenger), free local and on-campus phone calls

Also Available

Substance-free, special-interest, and theme housing

Did You Know?

Xavier has **historically been a commuter campus**, but recent years have shown that more students are now living on campus. With the addition of the Commons Apartments in 2002 and plans for a new dorm to be built in the next several years, Xavier is expected to have the majority of its undergraduates housed on campus in the near future.

Students Speak Out On...
Campus Housing

{ **"Buenger, Kuhlman, the Commons, and the Village are nice. Avoid everything else, unless you'd like to live in Brockman for the social stuff."**

Q "Buenger is nice, but it can be a **complete social prison**."

Q "The dorms are **all nice, especially Buenger**. Even Brockman isn't that bad."

Q "The dorms range in different degrees of comfort and sociability. The honors dorm, Buenger Hall, is the most comfortable, with living rooms and two bathrooms. However, **quiet hours and the spread-out suites can prevent students from getting to know more people**. The most social, yet least comfortable dorm is Brockman, which is a traditional college dorm with communal bathrooms and small rooms. The other two dorms, Husman and Kuhlman, are suite-style rooms where two-person rooms share a common bathroom. They offer the best mix of comfort and sociability."

Q "The dorms are all really nice. They are **much better than the average school**. For the social aspect, I would encourage all freshmen to live in Brockman. Yes, there are community bathrooms, but they are cleaned by maids, and I never experienced a line or anything. It's more of a common living experience, and you get to meet tons and tons of people. Some people prefer Kuhlman, Husman, and Buenger for their suite-style living, but I lived in both Kuhlman and Brockman, and I much preferred the latter."

Q "How you would like the dorms all depends on your desire. For the community and traditional college experience, there is Brockman Hall, for just the frosh. For those who like a roomy, but more isolated living area, there is Buenger, and then there are Husman and Kuhlman for those who want something in between. While there is on-campus housing for juniors and seniors, it has been known to be hard to get, so a student should be prepared to move off campus after his sophomore year, if necessary. There are **a lot of apartments and houses nearby** off campus, and with enough time, a good deal can be found. Safety becomes a bigger issue, however."

Q "**Buenger Hall is an awful place to meet people**, but is very nice."

Q "All the dorms are pretty nice, but **Brockman is the only one with community bathrooms**. Kuhlman and Husman are the nicer dorms. I'd recommend either one of those."

Q "If you like to study, then Buenger is nice. If you like to socialize, I recommend the other three dorms. I would say **Kuhlman gives you the best combination of both lives, though**."

Q "**Everyone says to avoid Brockman**, but it's not that bad. The other dorms are pretty nice by comparison."

Q "Brockman is a **hole in the wall**."

The College Prowler Take On...
Campus Housing

One of the advantages of being at a smaller school is that housing is typically nicer than you would find at a major state university. At Xavier, you're usually in good shape, regardless of which of the dorms you end up in. The only all-freshman dorm is Brockman Hall, the oldest and most traditional dorm on campus. The rooms are the smallest on campus, and you share a bathroom with the entire wing, but this hasn't stopped the ground floor, or "the Pit," from becoming the most infamous living space on campus. Brockman is the place to find the closest thing to a traditional dorm experience that Xavier has to offer. Kuhlman and Husman Halls are a little less congested than Brockman, and many students like the idea of sharing a bathroom with only three other people, as opposed to thirty. Kuhlman and Husman are adjacent to each other and are popular among freshmen and sophomores alike. For even ritzier conditions, you can live in Buenger Hall, which is outfitted with four- and six-person suites complete with a living room and two bathrooms. Buenger is mostly freshman and sophomore honor students, as well as athletes. Xavier houses its upperclassmen on campus with the Village Apartments and the Commons Apartments. Staying on campus during the upperclassmen years and getting into these apartments, especially the Commons, can be a gamble, depending on your lottery number, which is drawn at the end of each semester.

Housing is always an issue at Xavier because of how quickly the campus is growing. Many upperclassmen were not pleased when sophomores started being let into the Village based solely on their lottery numbers. Priority disputes aside, Xavier generally has clean and safe dorms and apartments. Even Brockman, which is considered to be the most "college-like" of the dorms, has plenty of amenities. Compared to other universities, Xavier's housing facilities are most definitely above average.

B

The College Prowler® Grade on
Campus Housing: B

A high Campus Housing grade indicates that dorms are clean, well-maintained, and spacious. Other determining factors include variety of dorms, proximity to classes, and social atmosphere.

Off-Campus Housing

The Lowdown On...
Off-Campus Housing

Undergrads in Off-Campus Housing:
52%

Average Rent For:
Studio Apt.: $330/month
1BR Apt.: $380/month
2BR Apt.: $725/month

Popular Areas:
Cleaney Avenue
Dana Avenue
Hudson Avenue

For Assistance Contact:
www.xu.edu/commuter

Students Speak Out On...
Off-Campus Housing

> **"Off-campus housing is not convenient at all, because XU doesn't regulate it. The options are relatively cheap, though."**

Q "Off-campus housing kind of sucks. You're really going to get a **taste of urban living** if you don't live in certain areas."

Q "Housing around XU is **as convenient as it is anywhere else**."

Q "Housing off campus is very **easy to obtain if you start looking early enough**. There are plenty of houses in the neighborhood to lease during the school year. Almost all students who want on-campus housing can get it without much problem, so there are much less off-campus students to compete for the local off-campus houses."

Q "In some cases, **it is worth it to live off campus**, but it depends how close to campus you are. However, housing isn't too difficult to find if you look early."

Q "While there is on-campus housing for juniors and seniors, it has been known to be hard to get, so a student should **be prepared to move off campus after their sophomore year** if needed. There are a lot of apartments and houses nearby off campus and, with enough time, a good deal can be found. Safety becomes a bigger issue, however, if you decide to live near the Norwood or Over-the-Rhine areas."

Q "I think housing is nice—if you are within walking distance. You **don't have to have a meal plan**, and you don't have to deal with loud people in the dorms."

Q "For the first two years, I would recommend staying on campus. Moving off campus sophomore year, **you lose the chance to see all your friends in the dorm**. You'll miss them more than you know."

Q "I would say **live on campus for two years**. Your sophomore year, you will meet more new people and expand your group of friends. It's hard to do that if you live in a house with just four people, while everyone else in your class is living, eating, and working together every day on campus."

Q "Housing off campus, for the most part, is dreary and overpriced. Rich landlords suck money out of homeless college students. **Something must be done**!"

The College Prowler Take On...
Off-Campus Housing

With the new upperclassmen apartments built, many juniors and seniors are choosing to stay on campus. However, many students at X want the freedom of their own place after serving time in the dorms. There are plenty of apartments and houses close to campus that are available for students to rent, and there are even a few that the University owns. In many respects, living off campus is cheaper, especially if you don't purchase a meal plan. Some of the problems that come up are that many of the streets and neighborhoods surrounding campus are not nearly as safe as the campus itself. Chances are, if you ask anyone who has moved off campus, they'll probably tell you that they enjoyed having a place to call their own once they got settled in and figured out how to adjust from the sheltered dorm life. Of course, don't expect the cleaning lady to come to your off-campus abode every Thursday with a bottle of Lysol and a fresh batch of toilet paper.

While there are a multitude of places to look for an apartment, the choices aren't always the best. Oftentimes, students find themselves in older apartments that are a far cry from the plush dorms they are used to at Xavier. With the size of the student body outgrowing the number of on-campus apartments XU offers, more and more juniors, seniors, and even sophomores are finding themselves living on their own. The main problem with off-campus housing at Xavier is value. In other words, you don't always get what you pay for. In the long-run, the price between on-campus and off-campus housing (meal plans excluded) is about the same, so if you are just looking for a place to crash, staying on campus may not be a bad solution.

B-

The College Prowler® Grade on
Off-Campus
Housing: B-

A high grade in Off-Campus Housing indicates that apartments are of high quality, close to campus, affordable, and easy to secure.

Diversity

The Lowdown On...
Diversity

Native American:
Less than 1%

White:
84%

African American:
10%

International:
1%

Asian American:
2%

Unknown:
1%

Hispanic:
2%

Out-of-State:
37%

Most Popular Religions

Catholicism is the primary religion, due to the fact that XU is a Catholic Jesuit school. However, there are groups and organizations for just about every religion you could think of, where students can join to explore their faith.

Political Activity

Cincinnati is one of the most conservative cities in America. However, Xavier's campus is often accused of being a liberal hotbed. The fact of the matter is that many of the actual students at Xavier come from conservative backgrounds, but the most loudly voiced opinions are considered to be progressively liberal. Both sides of the issues, however, are voiced in student organizations such as the College Republicans and College Democrats.

Gay Pride

Xavier is generally a polite and tolerant place. Groups like the Xavier Alliance ensure that GLBT students are treated equally and have a voice in the campus community.

Economic Status

Xavier is a pricey place to go to school, so there is naturally going to be a major influx of upper-middle-class students. However, there are people from all types of backgrounds due to the large amount of financial aid Xavier gives.

Minority Clubs

There are a plethora of minority-focused clubs at Xavier which can be seen in full force on campus. Minority clubs such as the Black Student Association often sponsor and promote many of the activities on campus.

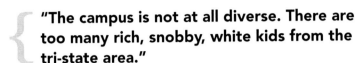

Students Speak Out On...
Diversity

"The campus is not at all diverse. There are too many rich, snobby, white kids from the tri-state area."

Q "We have maybe **100 African American students**. They tend to travel in large groups."

Q "Xavier **gives a ton of minority scholarships** to make the school look diverse, but it's not."

Q "The campus is not diverse at all compared to state schools. With the tuition as high as it is, **students at Xavier are predominantly white**. There are clubs for minorities, but they don't offer much culture to the all-too-white scene at Xavier."

Q "It is about **as diverse as you'd expect a private Jesuit school to be**."

Q "It's a mostly white student population, but you might not notice, because **everyone gets along very well**."

Q "My opinion is that this campus is diverse, especially due to its location in town. There are also **a lot of foreign students on campus**, but I don't know how to compare that to other universities, because I haven't spent enough time anywhere else to know."

Q "Xavier's **campus is really diverse**. Women are the majority, many Asian students are here, and African Americans are growing in population each year, too."

Q "Uh, the **campus is not very diverse**. We have a lot of Japanese exchange students, though."

Q "I think I **saw a Filipino once**."

The College Prowler Take On...
Diversity

Xavier's campus may technically be considered "diverse" when you look at the figures the school provides, but make no mistake: this is definitely middle America. While 48 foreign countries are represented in the student body, if you walk around campus, you'll find that probably accounts for close to 48 students. While kids from all across the country come to Xavier, the fact is that most of them have similar white, middle- to upper-class backgrounds. Also, the conservative political atmosphere at Xavier and surrounding Cincinnati doesn't invite much diversity either. If it's diversity you're looking for, Xavier may not be the ideal setting.

Xavier does its best to educate its students on diversity, even without actually experiencing much of it on a day-to-day basis. The wealth of minority clubs, such as the Black Student Association (BSA) and the speakers the University brings in from all over the world, help the middle-class white kids from the tri-state area to understand what life is like outside of the bubble that surrounds Xavier. Despite these efforts, Xavier is still not a very diverse place.

The College Prowler® Grade on
Diversity: D

A high grade in Diversity indicates that ethnic minorities and international students have a notable presence on campus and that students of different economic backgrounds, religious beliefs, and sexual preferences are well-represented.

Guys & Girls

The Lowdown On...
Guys & Girls

Men Undergrads:
44%

Women Undergrads:
56%

Birth Control Available?
No

Hookups or Relationships?

It's a well-known fact that every freshman girl on campus has a boyfriend either back home or at another school. It is also a well-known fact that, more often than not, this relationship doesn't survive past fall break. XU has an interesting mix of people just looking to hook up and people placing classified ads for their future spouse. There also seems to be a trend of students becoming engaged or married before graduation. However, the scene is dominated by the two major extremes: hookups and long-term relationships. Due to the fact that this is college, the former represents the majority.

Best Place to Meet Guys/Girls

Not blizzards, plagues, hurricanes, nor earthquakes can stop XU singles from pouring out of their dorms and heading to Soupie's, Dana's, and the off-campus parties on a weekly basis. While the chances of meeting Mr. or Mrs. Right are slim, you are almost sure to find Mr. or Mrs. "Right Now."

For those who aren't into the whole party and bar scene, many students will meet up through classes, clubs, or just in and around campus. With the on-campus community being so small, you are sure to be introduced to all your best friends' friends in no time. Taking in a movie or meeting up for lunch is a common way that XU coeds work their magic.

Dress Code

Xavier students will typically show up to class in whatever's clean that day. Actually, a lot of times it's not even that clean. Jeans, old T-shirts—anything goes on a day-to-day basis. There is a sizeable amount of students who actually "dress up" for class, wearing khakis, dress shirts, and clothes that have actually been washed rather than "Febrezed." During special occasions and weekends, girls are usually very dressed up. Guys, on the other hand, will usually wear whatever it is they wore to class, give or take a handful of hair gel and a polo shirt instead of a tee.

Did You Know?

Top Three Places to Find Hotties:
1. Soupie's
2. The quad when it's warm outside
3. The library, because brains count too

Top Places to Hook Up:
1. Soupie's
2. Off-campus parties
3. Your room
4. Pig Roast
5. Some vacant corner of the library once you find that brainy girl or guy

Students Speak Out On...
Guys & Girls

"The guys are, for the most part, obsessed with sports, while the girls are all Catholic and not very hot at all."

 "Most of the guys are jerks. The girls are either **prudes or just plain ugly**."

Q The **girls are getting hotter** and friendlier by the year."

Q "The guys and girls at Xavier are usually well dressed, and that is probably because of their general family income (upper-middle class to upperclass). Plenty of people take part in sports and clubs, so **many of the students are in good shape, as well**."

Q "The **freshman and sophomore girls seem to be quite nice**, but I haven't been on campus too much for socializing and the like."

Q "Well, I've heard from both sexes that the choices are somewhat, um, limited. I do know that there are more girls than guys, though, so **the guys have it better**. From what girls have told me, some guy they call Bobby Nachos is a nice catch."

Q "There are some pretty good-looking girls around. I've heard people say that there aren't a lot of hot girls here, but I disagree. Also, there are **a lot of girls here who actually have a personalit**, and who put some time into their academics, qualities which add so much more to this or that one hot girl."

Q "Most guys are pretty cool here. **You have your occasional hot shots who think they are God's gift** to the world. The girls have gotten better over the last couple of years since I've been here. As long as they continue the upswing, then I have no complaints."

Q "The people here **aren't exceptionally gorgeous**, and most of them honestly look the same. The school is overwhelmingly white, and everyone dresses in preppy clothing. Of course, like every college, the boys wear old T-shirts, faded hats, and cut-off cargos, but they are still pretty boys nonetheless. Girls here dress pretty conservatively. Lots of sweaters, oxford shirts, and khakis. They save the hoochie stuff for when they're shaking their behind at the bar."

Q "Everyday, I fall in love with five new girls I've never seen before. There is a fairly large number of extremely attractive girls on this campus. In addition, many of the same can even spell their names correctly and add and subtract. Seriously, though, the **girls here are attractive in mind, body, and soul**. I've met very many girls who are not only gorgeous, but also have high ambitions and are absolutely great conversationalists. I hope that one day one of them will talk to me."

The College Prowler Take On...
Guys & Girls

The student body at X is 56 percent female, so guys have the numbers in their favor. The girls at Xavier come in all different shapes and sizes. So whether you're looking for the girl next door or the girl with a strange piercing, chances are you'll find her; and regardless of whether you're looking for Miss Right or Miss Right Now, chances are, you'll at least find the latter if you're the social type. Some Xavier students proclaim that the girls and guys here all look the same due to the University's typical upper-middle socioeconomic class. However, in the looks department, the females at Xavier, for the most part, don't disappoint. On the plus side, most of them are capable of having an intelligent conversation, too!

As far as the guys go, a female Xavier student was once overheard proclaiming the following: "There are four types of guys at Xavier: taken, ugly, gay, and just plain loser." That's not exactly a fair assessment, based on the fact that, every weekend, plenty of the female coeds seem to find a way to look beyond those four stigmas and hook up anyway; that's just the way of the world—well, the college world anyway. The dating scene at X is lacking mainly because, for the most part, there are only two extremes: drunken hookups and marriage. If you're looking for something in between, good luck.

The College Prowler® Grade on
Guys: B-

A high grade for Guys indicates that the male population on campus is attractive, smart, friendly, and engaging, and that the school has a decent ratio of guys to girls.

The College Prowler® Grade on
Girls: B

A high grade for Girls not only implies that the women on campus are attractive, smart, friendly, and engaging, but also that there is a fair ratio of girls to guys.

Athletics

The Lowdown On...
Athletics

Athletic Division:
NCAA Division I

Conference:
Atlantic 10

School Mascot:
The Musketeer

Males Playing Varsity Sports:
128 (9%)

Females Playing Varsity Sports:
103 (6%)

→

Men's Varsity Sports:

Baseball
Basketball
Cross-Country
Golf
Rifle
Soccer
Swimming
Tennis
Track & Field

Women's Varsity Sports:

Basketball
Cross-Country
Golf
Rifle
Soccer
Swimming
Tennis
Track & Field
Volleyball

Club Sports:

Baseball
Boxing
Crew
Fencing
Lacrosse
Martial Arts
Mountaineering Club
Rugby
Running
Soccer
Volleyball
Ultimate Frisbee
Water Polo

Intramurals:

Basketball
Bowling
Floor Hockey
Coed Flag Football
Coed Softball
Flag Football (Men's)
Soccer (Coed)
Soccer (Men's)
Softball (Men's)
Tennis (Men's)
Racquetball
Volleyball

Athletic Fields

Intramural softball fields, intramural soccer field, tennis courts

Getting Tickets

Getting tickets to any event is free and relatively easy. Men's basketball is the only ticket you will have to wait in line for, and when XU plays Cincinnati, camping out is a requirement in order to secure your ticket for the Cross-town Shootout.

Most Popular Sports

Basketball and volleyball are the predominant attractions of Xavier athletics. Men's basketball and women's basketball have gained national recognition and have games broadcasted on ESPN, ESPN2, and FOX Sports Net. Volleyball is a popular spectator sport in the fall and winter, as well.

Best Place to Take a Walk

Ross Run located in the woods by the IM fields

Gyms/Facilities

Cintas Center

The Cintas Center is home to the men's and women's basketball teams, as well as the volleyball team. It contains a main floor in the 10,250-seat bowl where the big time action goes down. There is also an auxiliary gym where the basketball and volleyball teams hold their practices. The Cintas Center also is home to the dining hall, conference center, and a number of University offices, including the athletic department.

O'Connor Sports Center

The OSC is home to two large weight rooms, one with free weights and the other with Nautilus machines. Also available are a plethora of exercise bikes and treadmills for your cardio needs. In addition, there are three basketball courts, one of which is converted into a jazzercise/aerobics area during classes. The swim team competes in the Olympic-sized pool at the OSC, but it is open to students during normal operating hours.

Students Speak Out On...
Athletics

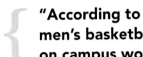

{ **"According to much of the student body, men's basketball is the only varsity sport on campus worth watching."**

Q "Basketball is life for a lot of folks. Intramural basketball is huge, too. Come to think of it, **people here are just basketball crazy**."

Q "Varsity sports aren't that big at all, not even basketball. **The fans are way too fickle**. IMs are moderately big, but nothing to write home about."

Q "Basketball is the main staple of Xavier University. Unfortunately, the other sports at the school do not get much recognition. The **intramural sports range through many popular sports** and give students the chance of competing in different leagues at different levels of competition. The IM department offers two levels of basketball, floor hockey, softball, and soccer."

Q "IM sports are big. It seems like **everyone is involved in some way**. The only varsity sport you need to know is basketball."

Q "Intramural sports are a whole lot of fun. I play at least one each season. They're competitive enough to get a good game, but relaxed enough to have fun at the same time. As for varsity sports, the lack of a football program makes our basketball team the focus of all attention. The **Cross-town Shootout and the Dayton games are the big ones**."

Q "Varsity basketball is probably the biggest event on campus. There is **no football team**, unlike most colleges. I would say more than half, if not most, of the campus is involved in some kind of intramural or club sport, which are fairly popular outside of the basketball season."

Q "Men's basketball is huge here on campus. The other sports seem to pull their weight as well. **IM sports seem to attract a lot of attention** as well."

Q "Basketball is the biggest. It is an awesome time, even the smaller games. The **intramurals are really fun, too**."

Q "The **only sports people pay attention to are basketball and volleyball**. I don't know about IM."

Q "Men's basketball is certainly the main draw for varsity sports on campus. While Xavier has many other male and female varsity sports such as soccer, volleyball, and baseball, not one garners as much University or student support as basketball. Though **students receive free admission to most varsity sporting events**, men's basketball games (especially the first home game and the Cross-town Shootout with the University of Cincinnati) are the only games that draw any sizeable crowd. Xavier has established a club known as the 'X-treme Fans,' which is devoted to supporting varsity athletics."

Q "The **basketball team is huge**. The students get free tickets to all the home games, and a large number of students are always present at them. Intramural sports are pretty popular."

The College Prowler Take On...
Athletics

Sports, both varsity and IM, are a big part of life on campus. While Xavier is a relatively small school enrollment-wise, the Musketeers have a big time athletic program. There are 14 NCAA Division I teams, so a large portion of the student body are athletes in some respect. The men's basketball team is the crown jewel of Xavier athletics. Selling out every home game in the 10,250-seat Cintas Center, students and alumni make home games the highlights of the week during the frigid winter months. The annual Cross-town Shootout against the University of Cincinnati is the hottest ticket in town, and it is also one of the biggest rivalries in college basketball. The sad fact is that other sports, such as the rifle team, are among the best in the nation, but little attention is paid to anything else but hoops. Als,o note that the school has been without a varsity football team since 1973. Aside from varsity sports, the intramural and club programs at X are popular and well organized. Flag football, softball, basketball, and volleyball are some of the more popular IM sports. Club sports such as rugby, lacrosse, and soccer are also popular for those looking for more intense competition.

The fact that Xavier does not have a football team hurts the athletic atmosphere on campus. However, during basketball season, there is no better place to be in the NCAA than at Xavier, with nationally-recognized men's and women's programs. Even the teams that do not get due exposure are competitive within their respective sports. Intramurals are widely popular and well organized, making Xavier a great place to catch a game or participate in one yourself.

A-

The College Prowler® Grade on

Athletics: A-

A high grade in Athletics indicates that students have school spirit, that sports programs are respected, that games are well-attended, and that intramurals are a prominent part of student life.

Nightlife

The Lowdown On...
Nightlife

Club and Bar Prowler:
Popular Nightlife Spots!

Since many Musketeers consider Soupie's a "club" as well as a "bar" (see below), they tend to gravitate there simply because it's close. For a different atmosphere that doesn't involve so many XU students or Norwood locals, these are a couple places that people will head to on special occasions, or when they just want to get away from campus.

Club Crawler:
Metropolis

125 Forest Fair Drive
Forest Park

(513) 671-2881

www.cincymetropolis.com

Metropolis is a triumvirate of clubs in the Forest Fair Mall: Rodeo's, a country music dance bar; the Underground, a techno club; and the Matrix, specializing in the latest pop and hip-hop tunes. The club is 21-and-over on Saturdays and Thursdays.

→

(Metropolis, continued)

Fridays and Sundays are 18-and-over. This allows all XU students to show up for contest night on Thursdays (Wet T-shirt, Best Butt—you get the idea), Mardi Gras Night on Fridays, and Ladies Night on Sundays. Metropolis is your typical bump-and-grind night club, with average prices, and a young, energetic atmosphere. For Xavier students who enjoy a good club scene, Metropolis is worth the drive off campus.

Red Cheetah

1133 Sycamore Street
Downtown

(513) 684-9500

The Red Cheetah is a high-energy dance club that bills itself as a premiere club, with lines of club-goers waiting to get in nearly every weekend night. The draw? It has an uptown club feel, with a mix of high-energy dance tunes ranging from techno-pop to hip hop combined with intimate, VIP seating areas. Bold red carpet and cheetah motifs everywhere give the club a wild flavor that attracts the 20-something crowd. The place is spacious, offering plenty of room to dance and mingle.

Bar Prowler:

The bar scene at XU revolves around the three dives within walking distance of campus. There are plenty of high-class establishments in driving distance and downtown, but for people who do their laundry with quarters and eat Ramen noodles for every meal, the local spots are all that matter.

Dana Gardens "Dana's"

1832 Dana Ave., Evanston

(513) 631-2337

www.danagardens.com

Dana's is the favorite hangout of Xavier's older crowd. While it's tastefully worn down, aka a dive bar, Dana's is steeped in tradition and familiarity. Most of these regulars are XU students, past and present, who enjoy the simpler things in life, namely a cold beer and a Muskie burger. With a second level with an outdoor deck available for when things get really crowded, Dana's is the epitome of a local college bar. Whether you are up for darts, drinking, eating, or just acting like a drunken idiot (an XU pastime), Dana's has you covered.

Norwood Café "The Woods"

3765 Montgomery Road
Norwood

(513) 631-1681

The Woods is another favorite among the "big three" dive bars in walking distance from campus. Slightly more worn down and a little more favored by the locals than Soupie's or Dana's, the Woods is an extremely laid-back place to sit and have a drink with friends. With $2 drafts being the standard and the chill atmosphere as the norm, the Woods is the place to go for the over-21 crowd to get away from the bells and whistles of Soupie's and relax in a more traditional bar-type atmosphere. One little known fact is that Charles Manson said that if he had a day out of prison, he would go to the Norwood Café and have a drink. Here's to hoping you're not there on that day.

Soupie's Grill and Bar

3861 Montgomery Road
Norwood

(513) 731-8156

This bar/grill/nightclub is located in walking distance from Xavier's campus and is extremely popular among the younger XU crowd. Aside from the sheer proximity, drink specials don't hurt, either. Tuesday night is Karaoke night, along with $2 Big A$$ Beers (22 oz. domestic bottles). On Wednesday nights, tons of Musketeers start the weekend early with college night, filled with 50-cent drafts and cheesy dance music all night long. Chances are, XU police will be sitting at the edge of campus, so don't do anything stupid while stumbling back to your dorm. The weird mix of Xavier kids and Norwood locals often provides some comical scenes if nothing else.

Student Favorites:

Dana Gardens

Norwood Café

Soupie's Grill and Bar

Useful Resources for Nightlife:

www.digitalcity.com/cincinnati/bars

www.cincinnatiafterdark.com

Bars Close At:

2 a.m.

Primary Areas with Nightlife:

Covington

Clifton

Downtown

Newport

Norwood

Cheapest Place to Get a Drink:

Norwood Café

Soupie's Grill and Bar

Local Specialties:

Burger

Christian Moerlein

Hudepohl

Little Kings

Favorite Drinking Games:

Beer Guy

Beer Pong

Card Games

Power Hour

House Parties

House parties at Xavier make up a large chunk of the nightlife. Houses on Dana, Marion, Clinton Springs, Shuttlesworth, and Hudson serve as the main hotspots for parties. During different points in the year, you can find the typical college "theme" parties, such as Halloween and the ever-so-rare toga party. If you're not sure where to go, you can always hang out at the shuttle stop at Ledgewood Circle and find out where everyone is headed. Most parties aren't too large, due to the fact that anything that spills outside or makes a lot of noise will be heard by the neighbors, who may, in turn, call the police. The north side of campus, which is technically in Norwood, has a "disorderly house" ordinance in place that keeps the larger parties to a minimum. The one party that is not to be missed is the Pig Roast, which occurs on the last Saturday before finals and shuts down almost the entire campus. Nearly everyone on campus gathers at a house on Fred Shuttlesworth Drive and engages in an all-day blowout featuring mud wrestling, the roasting of an actual pig, beer, and well, more beer. The event has become so big that wristbands are sold to gain entry, along with novelty T-shirts to commemorate the event.

What to Do if You're Not 21

Bogart's

2621 Vine Street

Corryville

(513) 281-8400

Bogart's is less of a club and more of a concert venue these days, bringing in the biggest names in alternative rock and hip hop. Holding about 1,000 people at most, the larger shows, such as Dashboard Confessional, sell out immediately. People from UC, Xavier, and northern Kentucky come out to see their favorite acts and enjoy the "rock club" feel that Bogart's has to offer. Tickets are usually between $10–$20, depending on the act, but it is always well worth it. Bogart's is located next to Buzz Coffee Shop, so you can go and decompress after being rocked all night long. Almost all the shows are for all ages, and anyone is welcome if they are into the music. Check *www.bogarts.com* for a detailed schedule of upcoming events.

The Buzz Coffee Shop and CD-O-Rama

2900 Jefferson Avenue

Corryville

(513) 221-3472

Buzz is definitely one of the hottest places to be near campus. Only a short drive away, this coffeehouse/CD store is a great place to hang out, relax, and talk with friends. Serving all kinds of interesting cappuccino and coffee mixes, Buzz caters to the sense of taste, as well as the sense of hearing. Buzz is a great place to be late at night as well, especially if you're tired of loud dance music and people spilling beer all over you. The store has plenty of couches and tables, and usually isn't too crowded, depending on what time you go. If you're looking for a rare used CD, or want to chill and listen to pretentious indie rock, Buzz is your place.

Hours: Monday–Friday 8 a.m.–2 a.m.

Saturday–Sunday 11 a.m.–2 a.m.

Organization Parties

Many organizations will plan nights out to restaurants or to a Reds game, but as far as partying goes, most clubs leave that to the general student body. Unless of course you count the rugby team as a student organization, in which case, yes, they do throw parties.

Frats

See the Greek section!

Students Speak Out On...
Nightlife

> "Parties on campus are not at all fun. There are too many people crowded into small spaces, and usually they get broken up by the cops before 11 p.m. Also, there are too few parties each weekend. Off-campus nightlife is bad. Dana's is way overrated."

Q "The parties are kind of lame. They are usually crowded and **cost a few bucks to get in**. Soupie's is a trashy bar, but it can be a decent time. No ID? No problem."

Q "The party scene on campus is very typical for a small college. The **bar scene in the area is pretty terrible**."

Q "The parties are nothing special. The larger ones usually consist of three kegs at the most. They are usually off campus in houses that are about a five-minute walk away. There are not too many clubs in Cincinnati, and many people visit Newport, KY, which is a 10-minute drive south over the river. **Many students patronize Soupie's**, a local bar located in nearby Norwood plaza. Also, Dana Gardens and the Woods are common college hangouts."

Q "Soupie's is where you want to be. Normally, the bouncers and bartenders are pretty lax in there, too. Dana's and the Woods are some good spots if you're over 21 (or if you have an ID from someone that is the same gender as you). Parties are alright for a while, usually anytime before November and after March you can find some good parties. **Winter parties are almost nonexistent**. After freshman year, it is much easier to find parties, but it definitely is possible for freshman to find them. I did."

Q "**Parties on campus aren't exactly every night** (though, I wouldn't know all of them anyway), but there are some. I haven't exactly frequented the clubs and bars off campus to know a whole lot about them, but there are some local places that people talk about all the time."

Q "Soupie's and Dana's are the personal favorites of the students. Anywhere on **Hudson is usually a good place for a party**."

Q "The parties are great, and I **love going to the bars**."

Q "Parties on campus are pretty rare, just because the campus police and the Norwood police are all about breaking them up before midnight. Most people go to the three dive bars around campus: the Woods, Soupie's, and Dana's. **Most parties are more like medium-sized gatherings of friends**, not huge ragers."

Q "I generally do not party on campus. I sit at home alone **drinking Natural Light** and reflecting on my failed life, while my dogs and my cat stare at me with disgust and shame."

The College Prowler Take On...
Nightlife

Most of the parties that take place normally happen off campus in the many houses and apartments inhabited by students. Any given weekend, one can find a party going on and, more often than not, Thursday and Sunday as well. The houses on Marion, Hudson, Clinton Springs, and Dana play host to the larger house parties. The residents of Norwood, the suburb that surrounds XU, often have had problems with student parties in the past, and they seem to have lobbied the police toward cracking down on large parties. The one large party that a natural disaster couldn't stop is the annual "Pig Roast." As far as bars and clubs go, Xavier students seem to gravitate to the closest havens possible. For freshmen and sophomores, the place to be is Soupie's, a bar and grill within walking distance of the dorms. While the younger crowd dances and drinks the night away at Soupie's, upperclassmen can often be found at Dana's. A local bar with a laid-back atmosphere, Dana's is a favorite of juniors, seniors, and kids who have laminated cards that say they're juniors and seniors. This same crowd can often be seen at the Woods, an even more dilapidated bar than Soupie's or Dana's, where the drinks are cheap and people such as Charles Manson have been regulars in the past. Still, others prefer to venture even closer to home and go to Ryan's Pub, which is conveniently located in the Gallagher Student Center. Sorry kids, those laminated cards don't work as well here.

Sadly, beyond the three dive bars and scattered house parties, there is not much to do on the weekends as far as nightlife. Due to the campus' distance from downtown, it takes a special occasion or an arsenal of designated drivers to bring XU kids to the hot spots of the Cincinnati nightlife. Once you find your niche, whether it be the bar scene, the party scene, or the sit-in-your-room-and-drink scene, you will realize the nightlife at Xavier is an acquired taste.

The College Prowler® Grade on
Nightlife: C+

A high grade in Nightlife indicates that there are many bars and clubs in the area that are easily accessible and affordable. Other determining factors include the number of options for the under-21 crowd and the prevalence of house parties.

Greek Life

The Lowdown On...
Greek Life

Number of Fraternities:
0

Number of Sororities:
0

Students Speak Out On...
Greek Life

{ **"There's a business frat, that's it. Frankly, I've been thinking of starting an egalitarian brotherhood, but keep that on the downlow."**

Q "There is **no Greek life**."

Q "There is zero Greek life here."

Q "The Greek life **pretty much doesn't exist**, as far as I know. There are a few fraternities that are somehow academic related, but I don't know a whole lot about them."

Q "There are no fraternities at Xavier. The closest thing is the rugby team which throws consistent parties and even has its own 'rugby house.' Other **club and varsity teams also have their own houses** and will frequently have parties."

Q "**Nonexistent**, unless you are black."

Q "Greek life is very limited since **purely social fraternities and sororities are forbidden** by the University. This being the case, Greek life clearly does not dominate the social scene."

The College Prowler Take On...
Greek Life

Greek life at Xavier is all but nonexistent. Being a Jesuit institution, you're more likely to find brothers wearing white collars and robes than brothers wearing wrinkled polo shirts and faded baseball hats. While a couple non-social frats do exist, such as an organization geared toward business majors, don't expect to find *Animal House* anywhere in the vicinity of Xavier's campus.

The overall lack of fraternities and sororities doesn't seem to bother too many XU students. The fact of the matter is, if they wanted to be in a Greek organization, they would've gone somewhere else. The smaller non-traditional fraternities have almost zero exposure on campus, making X more or less frat-free.

N/A

The College Prowler® Grade on
Greek Life: N/A

A high grade in Greek Life indicates that sororities and fraternities are not only present, but also active on campus. Other determining factors include the variety of houses available and the respect the Greek community receives from the rest of the campus.

Drug Scene

The Lowdown On...
Drug Scene

Most Prevalent Drugs on Campus:

Alcohol

Marijuana

Painkillers

Liquor-Related Referrals:

46

Liquor-Related Arrests:

3

Drug-Related Referrals:

2

Drug-Related Arrests:

0

Drug Counseling Programs

McGrath Health and Counseling Center

1714 Cleaney Avenue

(513) 745-3022

Services: Counseling services related to depression, anxiety, interpersonal problems, stress and time management, self-esteem, loneliness, anger, concerns about eating or body image, concerns about alcohol or drug use

Students Speak Out On...
Drug Scene

"As on any campus, there is the presence of drugs. From what I hear, marijuana is the drug of choice for the users, but some do take painkillers, and occasionally, even the harder stuff."

Q "There is a little pot around. I've heard **some drug dealers live near campus**."

Q "I don't know anything about it, so drugs **must not be that prevalent**."

Q "The drug scene **doesn't seem very big** at all."

Q "There **isn't any pressure to take drugs**. At a liberal arts college, everyone is cool with a person's personal choices. However, if you wanted to do that stuff, I guess it is possible."

Q "Actually, if there is a drug scene, I would say it is limited, or much hidden within certain groups, because I don't see a lot of it. There are **a number of people who spend some time with their alcohol**, though."

Q "I have **never found the drug scene to be a problem** with my studies or my social life."

Q "You can easily get weed if you want it, but **most people drink more than they smoke**."

Q "I've never touched the stuff, but I know that **it does exist at Xavier**."

The College Prowler Take On...
Drug Scene

One would be naïve to claim that drugs did not have a noticeable presence on campus. However, it's not like when walking from the student center to your dorm someone is going to offer you crack (although during finals week many people might consider searching for it). The drug scene is such that one can usually avoid it fairly effortlessly. Marijuana is clearly the narcotic of choice, based on what you'd see at a party and by reading the campus police notes in the school newspaper, and almost all students agree that heavier drugs such as coke or ecstasy are virtually nonexistent. While there is definitely a sizeable contingent of drug users on campus relative to the number of students, those choosing not to become involved are not hindered in their activities or harassed by others.

Whether people choose to indulge in drugs and alcohol is their own decision, and either way, you are still going to be respected at Xavier. If you were looking for drugs, chances are, you could ask around and find someone involved in the drug scene, but its visibility is so low that you could go about your normal daily routine without being exposed to drugs, and could even go to parties where alcohol is the only drug involved. It is safe to say that the drug scene qualifies as a seedy underbelly of the campus at best.

The College Prowler® Grade on

Drug Scene: A-

A high grade in the Drug Scene indicates that drugs are not a noticeable part of campus life; drug use is not visible, and no pressure to use them seems to exist.

Campus Strictness

The Lowdown On...
Campus Strictness

What Are You Most Likely to Get Caught Doing on Campus?

- Drinking underage
- Parking illegally
- Causing a noise disturbance in your dorm
- Trying to sneak into the cafeteria without getting your card swiped
- Stealing signs or parking cones
- Handing out flyers illegally

Students Speak Out On...
Campus Strictness

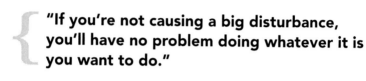

"If you're not causing a big disturbance, you'll have no problem doing whatever it is you want to do."

Q "Don't be foolish, and **you won't have a lot of trouble**."

Q "The police have been known to **cite underage drinkers on the shuttle** late at night and even students walking on campus drunk. The RAs and campus police will quickly break up dorm parties that have drugs or alcohol, fining the hosts."

Q "They're **pretty strict** about what goes on around campus."

Q "If campus police see any illegal substances, you're screwed, but they're not on the prowl for it everywhere. **Rule of thumb: don't be stupid**."

Q "Campus police are probably about **as strict as at most colleges**. However, I really wouldn't know, because I don't drink."

Q "Campus police are **quite strict at Xavier**."

Q "The campus police realize that people are going to drink. They won't just bust you for being drunk. **If you get rowdy or cause a scene, they will bust you**. As far as drugs, they will bust you for that, too."

Q "**Getting by at Xavier is just about being smart**. If you pass out on the green space in your own vomit, they're going to cite you. If you're walking down the hall with an open container, your RA will write you up. If you come home yelling 'I'm so drunk' you'll get in trouble. It's obviously illegal for people under 21 to drink, but it's also obvious that they will."

The College Prowler Take On...
Campus Strictness

While they would tell you otherwise, the unofficial policy of campus police seems to be "if we can't see it, and it's not bothering anyone, we'll let it slide." Drinking goes on in the dorms virtually every night to some degree, and as long as doors are shut and nobody is making any kind of disturbance, the campus police and Residence Life staff are fairly lenient. To those who do get caught, written warnings, fines, and double-secret probation await the not-so-wise. As for parties, the campus police usually have little, if any, jurisdiction for the larger parties which almost always take place off campus. The Cincinnati or Norwood police will usually put an end to things rather quickly if there are complaints of noise or if there are a lot of people wandering around on the front lawn. The one exception to this is the Pig Roast, the end of the year bash where Cincinnati's finest are there simply to make sure no one gets hurt. A general rule among Xavier students is: "don't act stupid, and you won't be cited."

Overall, it would be safe to say that the campus has a comfortable level of strictness. Campus police realize they cannot control every action each student takes, and they act accordingly. Potentially dangerous or annoying behavior is often shut down if it's in public, but there is nobody breathing down the student body's neck telling everyone what they can and cannot do. Most officers here look to protect students rather than punish them. Generally, the students feel safe and free to do whatever reasonable college activities they want.

B

The College Prowler® Grade on
Campus
Strictness: B

A high Campus Strictness grade implies an overall lenient atmosphere; police and RAs are fairly tolerant, and the administration's rules are flexible.

Parking

The Lowdown On...
Parking

Approximate Parking Permit Cost:
$140 ($100 for commuters)

XU Parking Services:
3868 Ledgewood Drive
(513) 745-1000
www.xu.edu/xucp

Student Parking Lot?
Yes

Freshmen Allowed to Park?
Yes

Common Parking Tickets:
Expired meter: $20
No parking zone: $50
Handicapped zone: $50
Fire lane: $100

Parking Permits

All students, faculty, employees and guests must have a valid parking permit at all times on campus.

Did You Know?

Best Places to Find a Parking Spot

- "The hill," also known as R-2
- Meters on Ledgewood
- South lot on Dana

Good Luck Getting a Parking Spot Here!

- The lower resident lot (R-1)

Students Speak Out On...
Parking

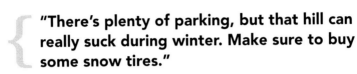

"There's plenty of parking, but that hill can really suck during winter. Make sure to buy some snow tires."

Q "Places to park at Xavier do exist, you just **have to drive around and look for them**."

Q "For resident students, there are **two available lots**. R-1, which is closest to the dorms and the classrooms, is full most of the time, and the best times to get a spot are late on a Friday or Saturday afternoon or when you've serendipitously caught someone leaving. A spot in R-1 is coveted and almost worn as a badge of honor. R-2, the parking lot used when R-1 is full (most of the time), is affectionately (and fittingly) referred to as "the hill," and about a five- to ten-minute walk from the dorms."

Q "Parking at Xavier is pretty horrible. I have to be honest, it's frustrating that a large number of the already limited spaces are reserved for people who rarely use them. Furthermore, parking becomes **even more limited when there is an event in the Cintas Center**. I don't know why they feel they must eliminate half the available spaces nine hours before the event, but they do it."

Q "There is **enough parking for everyone on campus**. There are two main residential lots for the students living in the dorms. Students will have to walk up a rather steep hill if they cannot find a spot in the lower lot. There is commuter parking all around the campus, and I have not heard any complaints about not being able to find a spot."

Q "It's easy to park, unless you mind being **out in the middle of nowhere**. Otherwise, it's crowded."

Q "The **parking situation at Xavier is hell**."

Q "Parking is not a problem. The **longest walk to your car might be 10 minutes**, if you were walking from all the way on the other side of campus."

Q "It's **not very easy to find parking**, unless you live in the Village. The Commons and the dorms are always packed, even on the weekends."

The College Prowler Take On...
Parking

Lack of adequate parking is one of the major gripes heard around campus. Most of the lots rest atop a large hill overlooking the layout of the campus, and unless you're lucky enough to grab a spot in one of the coveted lower lots such as R-1, it's going to be a long hike to wherever you're trying to go. Parking tickets and fines at and around Xavier are as steep as the hill on R-2, ranging from $20 to $50! However, the parking is well organized, with designated lots for residents and commuters and corresponding stickers that ensure everyone parks where they're supposed to.

Luckily, even if you park your car what seems like light-years away from where you need to be, the campus police will make sure it's safe. Positioning patrol cars in the parking lots after dark, the police make their presence felt to thwart any would-be window-smashing stereo thieves. There are also cameras near all of the on-campus lots, making it even harder for such vandals to ruin your day.

B+

The College Prowler® Grade on

Parking: B+

A high grade in this section indicates that parking is both available and affordable, and that parking enforcement isn't overly severe.

Transportation

The Lowdown On...
Transportation

Ways to Get Around Town:

On Campus
XU Shuttle Service

7:30 a.m.–2 a.m. weekdays and 7:30 a.m.–3 a.m. weekends

(513) 745-3748

Public Transportation
Southwest Ohio Regional Transit Authority

www.sorta.com

This agency provides reliable bus services in and around the city. Sometimes, though, the public transportation system often proves challenging to XU students: fares and schedules fluctuate daily, and standing out in the cold weather is not at all pleasant. If you plan to take buses, contact SORTA for current route schedules, maps, and rates. The Metro also operates a downtown and special events shuttle.

→

Taxi Cabs

A Taxi
(513) 771-4045

Yellow Cab
(513) 542-1450

Car Rentals

Alamo
local: (859) 746-6400
national: (800) 327-9633
www.alamo.com

Avis
local: (513) 793-7715
national: (800) 831-2847
www.avis.com

Budget
local: (513) 351-6137
national: (800) 527-0700
www.budget.com

Dollar
local: (866) 434-2226
national: (800) 800-4000
www.dollar.com

Enterprise
local: (513) 731-3131
national: (800) 736-8222
www.enterprise.com

Hertz
local: (513) 771-3518
national: (800) 654-3131
www.hertz.com

National
local: (513) 671-7807
national: (800) 227-7368
www.nationalcar.com

Best Ways to Get Around Town

Be adventurous, ride the Metro

Ride with a friend

Walk or bike

Ways to Get Out of Town:

Airlines Serving Cincinnati

American Airlines
(800) 433-7300
www.aa.com

Continental
(800) 523-3273
www.continental.com

Delta
(800) 221-1212
www.delta.com

Northwest
(800) 225-2525
www.nwa.com

TWA
(800) 221-2000
www.twa.com

US Airways
(800) 428-4322
www.usairways.com

Airport

Cincinnati/Northern Kentucky International Airport

(859) 767-3501

The airport is technically in Kentucky across the river. It is about 15 miles away and is a 20-minute drive from campus.

How to Get to the Airport

Bumming a ride is your best bet. The airport shuttle does not make regular trips to Xavier, so if you absolutely can't find a ride, the Metro would be your best choice. A cab service is also an option.

A cab ride to the airport costs about $25.

Greyhound

The Greyhound station is located at 1005 Gilbert Avenue, downtown. For scheduling information, visit *www.greyhound.com* or call (513) 352-6012. Student discounts are available.

Amtrak

1301 Western Avenue
Queensgate

(800) 872-7245

www.amtrak.com

Train tickets can be purchased through Amtrak for as low as $45 a person for trips to Chicago, Pittsburgh, New York, or Detroit.

Travel Agents

AAA Cincinnati Travel Agency

2712 Erie Avenue
Hyde Park

(513) 321-1222

R And South Travel

250 Grandview Drive
Fort Mitchell, KY

(859) 331-3500

Students Speak Out On...
Transportation

"Public transportation in Cincinnati is virtually nonexistent. There is the Metro bus system, which travels downtown and out to many of the city's suburbs, but, unless you have a good hour to spare, it's hardly convenient."

Q "The city of Cincinnati and Xavier both **have good transportation systems**."

Q "It's **not very convenient to get around town**. The shuttle service is nice, though."

Q "**Transportation is of no convenience** here. This is Cincinnati, after all."

Q "The bus is the most non-utilized method of transportation in the city by students. On the weekends, **fares are as low as 50 cents**. There is not a subway in Cincinnati, so the bus is the only public transportation. Many on-campus students have cars which they use rather frequently."

Q "Well, for just about a two mile radius around campus, **the shuttle is great to get to and from parties**."

Q "Aside from the shuttle service, which is very useful, most people just **find someone who has a car on campus** to go places."

Q "Never really used it, but **there are SORTA buses everywhere**."

Q "**It's not that great**. There is a bus, but I have never taken it."

Q "Transportation is **not very convenient**. I recommend finding a friend with a car."

The College Prowler Take On...
Transportation

The University provides a shuttle service that will take you anywhere on campus and a few blocks off campus, but, beyond that, there is not much in the way of public transportation. A plan for building a light-rail system in the Cincinnati area, which would have included a stop within walking distance of Xavier's campus, was shot down by the residents of Hamilton county, so no plans for improvement seem imminent. The Cincinnati buses are hardly used by students, due to the location of the bus stops and the general inconsistency of the city's mass-transit system. If you're looking to go somewhere off campus, your best bets are walking or finding a friend with a car.

Transportation can be a big problem in Cincinnati if you don't have a car or a friend who doesn't mind driving. The general opinion of the students is that the Metro is slow and unreliable. Also, some students show concern over taking the Metro because of the sketchy people that sometimes frequent the buses. For getting in and around campus, however, the shuttle service serves its purpose well. There are a couple places within walking or biking distance, but if you're looking to see something other than Norwood Plaza, you're going to need a car. The lack of a reliable public transportation system for students makes exploring the city inconvenient and unappealing for those without a car.

B-

The College Prowler® Grade on

Transportation: B-

A high grade for Transportation indicates that campus buses, public buses, cabs, and rental cars are readily-available and affordable. Other determining factors include proximity to an airport and the necessity of transportation.

Weather

The Lowdown On...
Weather

Average Temperature:

Fall: 57 °F
Winter: 34 °F
Spring: 55 °F
Summer: 75 °F

Average Precipitation:

Fall: 3.11 in.
Winter: 2.67 in.
Spring: 3.93 in.
Summer: 3.47 in.

Students Speak Out On...
Weather

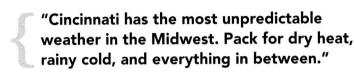

"Cincinnati has the most unpredictable weather in the Midwest. Pack for dry heat, rainy cold, and everything in between."

Q "It's kind of cold here. Make sure you **bring a jacket and gloves for the winter**."

Q "**Four seasons** can sometimes be seen all in the span of a day."

Q "It's **hotter than hell here**. Then it will rain for about six months, with brief interludes of bitter cold."

Q "Cincinnati **weather is extremely fickle**. It would be wise to bring clothing for all types of weather. The summer and spring tend to be very hot and humid, and the fall and winter get pretty cold and windy."

Q "The weather in Cincinnati sucks. **It seems like it rains every day**, however, the temperatures are similar to those of the middle-Atlantic seaboard (hot summer, cold winters, temperate falls and springs). There is not a substantial amount of snow since Cincinnati is not close to the lake effects of Cleveland."

Q "Shorts can usually be worn all through September. Once October comes, however, be ready to wear sweatshirts and jeans. Then, **in the winter, a heavy coat might be necessary**."

Q "Right now, it's terribly hot, but the winters are formidable. **Common sense will serve you well** in this department."

Q "The weather is hot in the summer and cold in the winter, with about a week of decent weather in between, so **bring a wide range of clothing**."

Q "The **weather stays warm until October** and gets warm again in the middle of March. A heavy coat is advisable for the winter and so are many long clothes once it starts to cool off."

Q "It's humid in the summer. Really windy and cold in the winter, but **not much snow**."

The College Prowler Take On...
Weather

Cincinnati's weather is an anomaly, kind of like Mother Nature's little freak experiment. It can be rainy and 40 degrees one day, then sweltering hot and 85 degrees the next. Regardless of the time of year, any kind of weather is possible on any given day. Be a good Boy or Girl Scout, and come prepared for anything. Be sure to bring all types of clothing for all seasons. The winters are usually frigid, but lacking in the snow department compared to the rest of Ohio. Freezing rain is a regular occurrence, so come with plenty of cold medicine in anticipation of the campus-wide epidemic of sickness that frequently spreads sometime around finals. Once winter does finally subside, the last few weeks of school usually welcome a refreshing burst of sunny skies, warm weather, and tank tops. With plenty of green space in the heart of campus, make sure to bring a football, Frisbee, or beach towel, because the quad is the place to be once the weather gets warm.

People in Cincinnati seem obsessed with their weather because of how weird it is. Some even take pride in being able to deal with the sporadic conditions year after year. Honestly, after living here for a while, you can't blame them. The unpredictability can be a hassle, and it seems like there are no definitive seasons to dress for. Unless tear-away pants come back into fashion, getting dressed in the morning in Cincinnatie is a gamble most of the year.

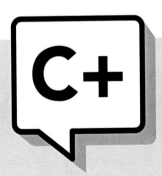

C+

The College Prowler® Grade on
Weather: C+

A high Weather grade designates that temperatures are mild and rarely reach extremes, that the campus tends to be sunny rather than rainy, and that weather is fairly consistent rather than unpredictable.

Report Card Summary

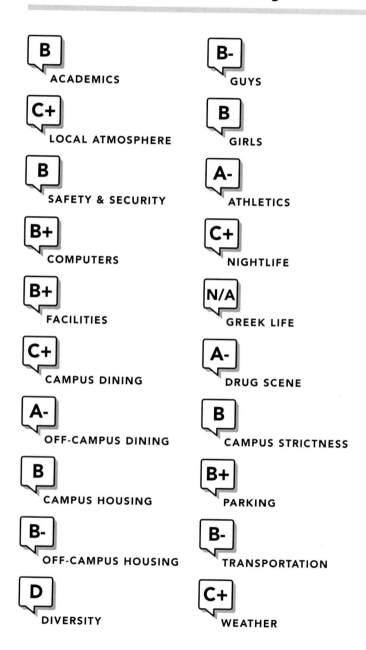

B — ACADEMICS

C+ — LOCAL ATMOSPHERE

B — SAFETY & SECURITY

B+ — COMPUTERS

B+ — FACILITIES

C+ — CAMPUS DINING

A- — OFF-CAMPUS DINING

B — CAMPUS HOUSING

B- — OFF-CAMPUS HOUSING

D — DIVERSITY

B- — GUYS

B — GIRLS

A- — ATHLETICS

C+ — NIGHTLIFE

N/A — GREEK LIFE

A- — DRUG SCENE

B — CAMPUS STRICTNESS

B+ — PARKING

B- — TRANSPORTATION

C+ — WEATHER

Overall Experience

Students Speak Out On...
Overall Experience

> "I really like it here, mostly because of the friends I have made, including some of my teachers. Although I sometimes wish the school were a little bigger, or Cincinnati was more entertaining, I enjoy it."

Q "I sometimes **wish I was somewhere else**. The electronic media major is a joke if you don't want to go into television."

Q "I am enjoying Xavier very much. **The friends that I have made are great**, and I am involved with many clubs and organizations. I wish that I was a little closer to home sometimes. However, it is nice to be able to be on my own and have a little independence."

Q "I love it here at Xavier and **would not trade it for any other school**. I have great teammates on the cross-country team, and I have made many great friends."

Q "My overall experience has been great. **I love the school's enthusiasm for all of its endeavors**. There is also something for everyone. The clubs and organizations make it very easy to meet many people with the same beliefs, goals, and ideals as you. I really feel like I'm in a place that cares personally about my development and takes serious steps to ensure that I succeed not only here, but throughout the rest of my life, as well."

Q "Sometimes, I wish I had gotten in somewhere else, but for the most part, my experiences have been overly good. **I'm glad that I chose Xavier for my education**."

Q "I'm glad I picked Xavier. **I've never had so much fun in my life**. I've met some awesome people and did some cool stuff along the way. I stand by my decision 100 percent."

Q "I really like Xavier because of the **personal interaction in the classes** and the amount of help that professors are willing to give. With this in mind, I love being here, as I am absolutely focused on my academics and where they will take me. Most everyone here is very friendly and outgoing. But, I do think that whether or not this is the right school for someone all depends on the personality of that student."

Q "**I love it at Xavier** and wouldn't change it for the world."

Q "**I sometimes wish I went to a bigger school**, but it's kind of fun to know most people at parties or to know a lot of faces when you're walking to and from class."

Q "This **school is kind of lame**. I sometimes wish I went to Ohio State or Dayton."

The College Prowler Take On...
Overall Experience

Overall, I am definitely satisfied with my experience at Xavier so far. Adjusting to a new city, new school, and new friends was tough at first, but in retrospect, if I were somewhere else besides Xavier, it would've been a lot tougher. The combination of a small school where you can get to know everyone with a big-school atmosphere, including big-time college sports and a big city to explore, makes Xavier a fun and interesting place to be. The people at Xavier are really some of the friendliest you'll meet. (As tired as that sounds, it's absolutely true.) The reason that Xavier has such a high retention rate is that people who take an honest look at Xavier normally want to go here, and rarely are they let down. It's clear when you visit here that things are laid-back, there are no gigantic parties on a weekly basis, and everything is in general serene and comfortable. While it may differ from the typical college experience portrayed in all our favorite movies, the XU experience is enjoyable and dynamic. The beauty of X is it can be whatever you choose to make it. At another school, the pace of life is often determined by a gigantic student body, and if you don't conform, you are an outcast. At Xavier, students have the freedom to be individuals and study, work, and play just about any way they want to.

Sure, there are plenty of things you could gripe about The parking situation is a pain. Housing can be a hassle. Also, if you're looking for a major blowout party every single weekend, Xavier's probably not for you. However, during your tenure at Xavier, you will meet tremendous people from places and backgrounds you may never have been exposed to before, and you will also get opportunities, both academic and in life, that you could not have had anywhere else. Go Musketeers!

The Inside Scoop

The Lowdown On...
The Inside Scoop

XU Slang:

Know the slang, know the school. The following is a list of things you really need to know before coming to XU. The more of these words you know, the better off you'll be.

ALL Card – Your student ID card. You need this for everything. Can also function as a USBank ATM card.

Dartanian – The statue of the famous Musketeer outside of the Cintas Center.

The G-Spot – The Gallagher Student Center.

Greenspace – Can be used in reference to any of the patches of grass on the Residental Mall.

The Hill or Up Top – The secondary residential lot, officially called R-2.

ISS – Information Systems and Services. These are the people who get blamed for everyone's computer troubles.

→

Kro-Ghetto – The Kroger grocery store located in the Norwood Plaza next to campus.

OSC – O'Connor Sports Center.

The Pit – The basement floor of Brockman Hall.

Res Mall – Short for "Residential Mall," a stretch of land that is occupied by the major dorms and the Gallagher Student Center.

The 'Tas or The X-Box – The Cintas Center.

The Woods – Norwood Café.

The X – The large letter X on the ground at the end of the Academic Mall.

Things I Wish I Knew Before Coming to XU

- Meeting people takes a lot of effort if you live in certain dorms.
- Only spend money on the bare essentials.
- Do not, I repeat, do not bring your high school yearbook.
- Overuse of Instant Messenger will reduce your GPA by at least 0.2, guaranteed.
- It's better to get some sleep and wake up early and finish work than to pull numerous all-nighters.
- Everyone acts like an idiot in college, so don't feel so bad.

Tips to Succeed at XU

- Go to class! Remember, 80 percent of life is just showing up.
- Be open to new ideas and experiences.
- Get in the habit of studying at the same time every night.
- As important as it is to study, having fun and relaxing can be just as crucial.
- Be thrifty. You will be astounded by how quickly you go through cash here.

XU Urban Legends

- The E! show "Wild On" was supposedly going to film a show at Soupie's.

- A man known as the Brockman Night Watcher allegedly watched girls in Brockman Hall while they slept a number of times, but was then apprehended.

- An XU dad bought the house across from Bellarmine Chapel so his daughter could live on campus.

- Xavier, a Catholic school, has more professors that are Jewish than any other religion.

- Xavier is getting a football team sometime in the near future.

School Spirit

Xavier students are definitely proud of their school, and it shows. With clubs like the X-Treme Fans in place to help promote athletic events, it is hard to miss the spirit that surrounds XU. While basketball is the primary sport for which students actually express their school spirit, when they do, it is as abundant as any place in the country. A good percentage of students also wear Xavier apparel and colors every day to class to show their pride in being a Musketeer.

Traditions

The Crosstown Shootout
The battle between Xavier and the University of Cincinnati has been going on since 1927, when Xavier, then an all-male institution, took on UC at the old Schmidt Field House and won, 29-25. The rest, as they say, is history. Every year, in the middle of basketball season, the entire town experiences a division of allegiance. The site of the Xavier–UC game, now known as the Skyline Chili Cross-town Shootout, rotates annually. Xavier has come out on top six out of the last ten times. Students have camped out all night and even have been known to skip a few classes until the tickets are distributed. The Shootout is broadcast annually on ESPN or ESPN2, and every bar in the city is packed with Cincinnati Bearcat and Muskie supporters alike, hoping for another victory in one of college basketball's most heated rivalries.

The Pig Roast
The annual Pig Roast is by far the best social event of the year for XU coeds. Not only does it commemorate the last week of classes for the year, but it also serves as an opportunity for everyone on campus to party one last time before summer. While no one is sure when the Pig Roast officially became its namesake, the idea of having a gigantic party at the end of the year is decades old. The event has become so big that the tenants of the house where it is held sell wristbands at 10 bucks a pop to get in, and they give out commemorative T-shirts as well. That way, when you wake up the next day and don't remember where you were, you can look at your shirt and say, "Oh!" It is a well-known fact that the Pig Roast is going to happen no matter what, so Cincinnati police officers show up to keep the peace and make sure no one gets hurt.

Finding a Job or Internship

The Lowdown On...
Finding a Job or Internship

When XU grads or soon-to-be grads want to find an internship or full-time employment, the Center for Career and Leadership Development will help you quickly narrow your job search into the most productive areas and present them to an eager community of employers. The CCLD, located in the Gallagher Student Center, coordinates on-campus employment as well as post-graduate job search assistance. Through the Web-based job posting system, soon-to-be graduates can learn about openings in their specific career areas and conduct their job search.

Career Center Stats

- 87 percent of recent graduates report that their job position is related to their major.
- 600 resumes are referred to employers every year.
- 3,000 jobs are listed on Xavier's Web-based job posting system every year.
- 2,000 students are helped by Xavier's Center For Career and Leadership development.

CCLD Web site: *www.xu.edu/careerandleadership*

Advice

Don't be afraid to start talking to CCLD about job opportunities as early as possible. Chances are they have connections to at least one company or internship program that could be beneficial that you wouldn't be able to secure on your own. Also, if you're looking to make a few extra bucks, don't be afraid to stop by and see what openings there are around campus.

Career Center Resources & Services

Job search

Internship coordination

Leadership development

On-campus employment

Orientation services

Grads Who Enter The Job Market Within

6-Months: N/A

1-Year: 69%

Firms That Most Frequently Hire Grads

AC Nielsen BASES, Children's Hospital Medical Center, Cintas Corp., Fifth/Third Bank, General Electric, Kroger Company

Alumni

The Lowdown On...
Alumni

Web Site:
www.xu.onlinecommunity.com

Office:
Alumni Center on
Dana Avenue

Services Available:
Job search
Mentoring programs
Short-term medical insurance
Travel programs
Updates on alumni
Xavier checking account
Xavier Visa card

Major Alumni Events

The largest events the Alumni Association is involved in are Homecoming and the reunions that take place on campus toward the end of the school year. There are also alumni chapters for each region, which hold several events a year, including trips to baseball games, cookouts, open houses, and other gatherings. Xavier has an alumni contingent of roughly 55,000.

Alumni Publications

Xavier Magazine is published quarterly and is sent out to all alumni, faculty, and parents of current Xavier students. It features alumni profiles, fundraising info, features, and general news to keep the alumni up to speed about what's going on at XU.

Did You Know?

Famous XU Alumni:

Jim Bunning (Class of '53) – Pitched a no-hitter for the Philadelphia Phillies, elected to the Baseball Hall of Fame, U.S. Senator for Kentucky (R).

Dr. Charles M. Geschke (Class of '62) – Co-founder and Chairman of the Board at Adobe Systems. Holds a PhD in computer science from Carnegie Mellon University, a MS in mathematics, and a AB in classics, both from Xavier University.

Janet Smith Dickerson (Class of '68) – Vice President of Princeton University.

John Dreyer (Class of '69) – Vice President, Walt Disney Co.

Ken Blackwell (Class of '70) – Ohio Secretary of State.

Ken Lucas (Class of '70) – U.S. Congressman from Kentucky (D), 4th District.

Tyrone Hill (Class of '90) – Former NBA player for the Philadelphia 76ers, named to the NBA All-Star Team in 1995.

Brian Grant (Class of '94) – Current NBA player for the Phoenix Suns, winner of the J. Walter Kennedy Citizenship Award for the 1998–99 NBA season in recognition of his outstanding community service and charitable work.

David West (Class of '03) – Current NBA player for the New Orleans Hornets, selected 18th overall in the 2003 NBA Draft.

Student Organizations

Academic Organizations

Accounting Society – Supports XU students who major in accounting.

Advertising Club – Group outside class for advertising majors and others interested to explore advertising issues, field trips, social events.

Alchemist Club – Facilitates the propagation of chemical knowledge and assists in making the chemistry major a viable option.

Alternative Break Club – Provides students with an opportunity to gain personal growth through education, direct service, and new experiences drug and alcohol free.

Amnesty International – Promotes awareness on human rights issues and opposes human rights abuses around the globe.

Archaeological Society – Promotes XU dedication to the study of ancient cultures and societies.

AUSA – Disseminates knowledge, promotes the efficiency of the United States Army.

Biology Club – Established to nurture an interest among the Xavier community in the biological sciences.

(Academic Organizations, continued)

Black Student Association – Events geared to black students; a venue to voice their concerns.

Brand X Videos

Circle K – Helps mold University students into responsible citizens with a lifelong commitment to community service.

College Democrats – Provides a voice for University Democrats and a forum for healthy political discussion.

College Friends – Seeks to pair XU students with local elementary schools. XU students are a role model and friend.

College Republicans – Dedicated to the principles of the Republican Party Platform.

Computer Science Club – Serves to educate interested users in various aspects of computing technology.

Earthbread – Creates awareness of hunger and food issues at the local, national, and international levels through a variety of events.

Earthcare – Raises environmental awareness and promote action on XU campus and Cincinnati community. *www.xu.edu/clubs/Earthcare.htm.*

Economics Club – Provides opportunities for students to learn applications of economics and recognize outstanding academic achievements in economics.

Education Club – Worldwide mission to improve educational outcomes for individuals with exceptionalities.

Entrepreneurial Club – Designed to inspire and serve as an incubator for new ideas, learn from others who have experienced the entrepreneurial world.

Finance Club – Educates its members to the possibilities a degree in finance makes available to them.

French Club – Increases awareness of the French culture and customs by offering fun, as well as educational activities to all students.

Gentlemen Organized for Achievement & Leadership (GO. AL) – "As African American men, we plan to take action and educate African American males and the community around academics, spirituality, community, culture, and progressive professionalism."

(Academic Organizations, continued)

Habitat for Humanity – Involves XU students who strive to eliminate poverty housing.

Heidelburg Club – Provides an interesting and enjoyable outlet for students interested in the German culture and language. *www.geocities.com/xudeutschklub*

Information Systems Club – Exists to provide IS majors contacts with professionals in this field and to interact with other universities in the IS field.

International Students' Society – Forum for international students to voice opinions on XU policies and activities.

Marketing Club – Offers students the opportunity to gain a broader, more realistic, more practically-oriented exposure to marketing activities.

Math Association of America – Promotes the interest of mathematics at XU. Aids students, promotes interaction among undergrads and faculty, and links students to worldwide community.

Mermaid Tavern – Provides an open and relaxed environment for writers to shape their work and seek guidance.

Music Education Club – Established to make available to members opportunities for professional development, become acquainted with education profession, assists XU music department on various projects.

Pax Christi – Established to work with all people for peace for humankind, always witnessing to the peace of Christ.

Physics Club – Informative activities to help students make decisions regarding their future in physics.

Pre-Law Society – Inform students about field of law, law school admission procedure, employment opportunities, and other related topics. *www.xu.edu/pre_law/club_info.html*

Pre-Med Society – Provides support and guidance to students planning to become a health professional. *www.xu.edu/clubs/premed.htm*

St. Peter Catholic Society – Aims to connect XU students with Catholic doctrine and traditions.

St. Vincent DePaul Society – Exists to provide students with the opportunity to perform faith-inspired service.

(Academic Organizations, continued)

Senior Board – *www.xu.edu/clubs/Senior%20Board/members.htm*

Senior Classical League

Ski Club

Spanish Club – Serves as an extension of the classroom and promote interest in Hispanic literature and culture.

Spirit Squad

Students for Life – Seek to open the XU community to the appreciation of the sanctity of human life from the moment to conception to natural death.

Students for Peace

Student Occupational Therapy Association (XU SOTA)

Student Organization Latinos (SOL)

Take Back the Night – Strives to create possibilities for women to envision and engage in a life that maximizes their potentials.

Voices of Solidarity (VOS) – Pledge to educate XU students and faculty regarding the grave political, economic, and social problems facing the nations of Latin America.

WRXC – Give students experience in electronic media via exposure to equipment and materials in a semi-professional environment.

Xavier Alliance – Provides a safe place for gay, lesbian, and heterosexual students to meet.

X-treme Fans – Promotes school spirit through participation in supporting XU's intercollegiate athletic teams.

Xavier Greens – Strives to represent the 10 key values of the Green Party: community-based economics, decentralization, ecological wisdom, feminism, future focus, grassroots democracy, non-violence, personal and global responsibility, and social justice.

XUSOFAT (athletic training) – Offers athletic training students a venue to learn, increase their professional skills, and have fun.

Social Organizations

Alpha Epsilon Delta – Encourages and recognizes excellence in scholarship within health sciences.

Alpha Kappa Alpha

Alpha Phi Alpha – Promote a more perfect union among men, to aid in and insist upon personal progress of its members.

Alpha Phi Omega – This fraternity assembles in the fellowship derived from the Scout Oath and law of the Boy Scouts of America.

Alpha Sigma Nu – Honors Society where students demonstrate an intelligent appreciation of and commitment to the ideals of Jesuit higher education—intellectual, social, moral, and religious.

Athenaeum – Proposed to publish the literary and artistic expressions of XU students.

Band – Development of the musical community: Band, Symphonic Wind Ensemble, Pep Band, Swing Band, Muskie Blues.

Chi Sigma Iota – International honor society for counselors in training, counselor educators, and professional counselors.

Concert Choir – Organization of musicians dedicated to the continuing education of the department of music through recruitment of musicians, development of talent, and community building.

Delta Sigma Pi – Fraternity organized to foster the study of business in universities; promote closer affiliation between the commercial world and students of commerce.

Delta Sigma Theta – Sorority chartered by XU 1992. Programs based on economic and educational development, international involvement, physical and mental health, and political awareness and involvement.

Eta Sigma Phi – Promote study and awareness of classical civilizations, also recognizes classics students for superior achievement.

Gospel Choir – Established to maintain a multicultural attendance, work together to minister through song, and enhance our musical abilities.

(Social Organizations, continued)

Jazz Ensemble – Committed to playing jazz, blues, funk, rock, and fusion at the highest aesthetic and artistic level possible.

Mortar Board – National honor society recognizes college seniors for their achievements in scholarship, leadership, and service; creates opportunities for continued leadership development.

Musketeer Annual – Annual student yearbook.

Newswire – Weekly student newspaper.

Pershing Rifles – Develop to the highest possible degree the outstanding traits of leadership, discipline, and military bearing within the framework of a military-oriented fraternity. Honor guard for the XU president.

Phi Alpha Theta – Promote historical studies at XU, promote historical interest, uphold interests and directions of national chapter.

Psy Chi Psychology Honors Club – Seeks to encourage, stimulate, and maintain excellence in its members in the area of psychology.

Sigma Gamma Rho

Sigma Pi Sigma

Singers

Student Working Groups

Board of Ambassadors

Muskies Own Recruitment Effort (MORE)

Peer Leadership Team

Student Alumni Association

STYUKA

X-Action

The Best & Worst

The Ten **BEST** Things About XU

1	Friendly and interesting people
2	The Crosstown Shootout
3	Food and housing are great
4	New student center
5	Extremely safe
6	Free tutoring for any subject
7	Good location and you can drive to just about anywhere
8	Easy to get a job
9	Liberal with giving scholarships and financial aid
10	Everyone can bring a car

The Ten **WORST** Things About XU

1 No strong sense of community around campus

2 Very limited nightlife

3 No football

4 Not very diverse

5 Parking up on the hill

6 No on-campus eats late at night

7 Norwood can be a shady area

8 Core classes are not the most interesting

9 The student center is nice and shiny, but lacks activites

10 Small classes also mean that registration can be a difficult at times

Visiting

The Lowdown On...
Visiting

Hotel Information:

Local:

Best Western Inn

8020 Montgomery Road
Cincinnati

(513) 793-4300

www.bestwestern.com

Distance from Campus:
2 miles

Price Range: Xavier rate
of $69

**Kings Island Resort &
Conference Center**

5691 Kings Island Drive
Cincinnati

(800) 727-3050

www.kingsislandresort.com

Distance from Campus:
5.5 miles

Price Range: Xavier rate
of $69

→

Quality Hotel & Suites

4747 Montgomery Road
Cincinnati

(513) 351-6000

800 292-2079

Distance from Campus:
1.5 miles

Price Range: Xavier rate
of $75

Staybridge Suites by
Holiday Inn

8955 Lakota Drive West,
West Chester

(513) 874-1900

*www.staybridge.com/
cincinnati*

Distance from Campus:
7 miles

Price Range: Xavier rates
starting at $89

The Vernon Manor Hotel

400 Oak Street,
Cincinnati

(800) 543-3999

www.vernonmanorhotel.com

Distance from Campus:
3 miles

Price Range: Xavier rate
of $69

Downtown:
Crowne Plaza

15 W. Sixth Street
Cincinnati

(513) 381-4000

*www.basshotels.com/
crowneplaza*

Distance from Campus:
15 minutes

Price Range: Ask for special
Xavier rate

Embassy Suites
River Center

Covington, KY

(859) 261-8400

www.embassysuites.com

Distance from Campus:
7 miles

Price Range: Xavier rate
of $129

Specialty:
Empty Nest Bed
and Breakfast

2707 Ida Avenue
Norwood

(513) 631-3494

Distance from Campus:
4 miles

Price Range: $89

Take a Campus Virtual Tour

See *www.xu.edu/virtual_tour* for details.

To Schedule a Group Information Session or Interview

Xavier schedules information sessions and interviews around the country as well as on campus. Contact the admissions office at (877) 982-3648 to find out when a representative will be in your area. If you are planning on visiting campus on an individual tour, an information session and tour are included.

Campus Tours

X Experience Days

Registration for an X experience day may be made by calling the office of admission at (877) XUADMIT or (513) 745-3301, Monday through Friday 8:30 a.m.–5 p.m. A confirmation including a parking pass, campus map, directions, and area accommodations will be sent to those who RSVP at least one week prior to the event.

Individual Tours

To set up an individual campus tour, contact the office of admission at (513) 745-3301, or Nancy Broxterman at broxter@xavier.edu. A two-week advance notice is requested.

The Club X program is intended for accepted high school seniors only. After being accepted to Xavier, you will receive an official invitation to Club X and a response form. The response form must be completed and sent back to the Office of Admission along with the $30 fee. Most Club X dates tend to fill up about one month in advance. Upon receipt of your response form, you will be notified of your selected date and given an official confirmation notice. If you have any questions or comments about the process, or if you would like an additional response form, contact the office of admission at (800) 344-4698 ext. 3301 or xuadmit@xavier.edu.

Directions to Campus

Driving from the North
- Take I-75 South toward Toledo.
- Take the US-42/ Reading Rd. exit.
- Turn right onto Reading Rd./ US-42.
- Follow the Xavier signs onto Victory Parkway.

Driving from the South
- Take I-75 North toward Lexington.
- Merge onto I-71 North via exit number 1A toward US 52 East/Columbus.
- Take exit number 5 toward Montgomery Rd./ Dana Ave.
- Turn right onto Duck Creek Rd.
- Turn right onto Montgomery Rd./ OH-3/ US-22.
- Turn left onto Dana Ave.
- Follow the Xavier signs onto Victory Parkway.

Driving from the East
- Take I-70 West toward Columbus.
- Merge on to I-270 South via exit 108A toward Cincinnati.
- Merge onto I-71 South via exit 55 toward Cincinnati.
- Take the Dana Ave. exit 5, turn right at the stoplight.
- Follow the Xavier signs onto Victory Parkway.

Driving from the West

- Take I-70 East toward Indianapolis.
- Merge onto I-74 Eeast via exit number 73A.
- Merge onto I-75 North via exit number 20 (on the left) toward Dayton.
- Merge onto OH-562 Eeast via exit number 7 toward I-71/ Norwood.
- Take the US-42/ Reading Rd. exit.
- Turn right onto Reading Rd./ US-42.
- Follow the Xavier signs onto Victory Parkway.

Words to Know

Academic Probation – A suspension imposed on a student if he or she fails to keep up with the school's minimum academic requirements. Those unable to improve their grades after receiving this warning can face dismissal.

Beer Pong/Beirut – A drinking game involving cups of beer arranged in a pyramid shape on each side of a table. The goal is to get a ping pong ball into one of the opponent's cups by throwing the ball or hitting it with a paddle. If the ball lands in a cup, the opponent is required to drink the beer.

Bid – An invitation from a fraternity or sorority to 'pledge' (join) that specific house.

Blue-Light Phone – Brightly-colored phone posts with a blue light bulb on top. These phones exist for security purposes and are located at various outside locations around most campuses. In an emergency, a student can pick up one of these phones (free of charge) to connect with campus police or a security escort.

Campus Police – Police who are specifically assigned to a given institution. Campus police are typically not regular city officers; they are employed by the university in a full-time capacity.

Club Sports – A level of sports that falls somewhere between varsity and intramural. If a student is unable to commit to a varsity team but has a lot of passion for athletics, a club sport could be a better, less intense option. Even less demanding, intramural (IM) sports often involve no traveling and considerably less time.

Cocaine – An illegal drug. Also known as "coke" or "blow," cocaine often resembles a white crystalline or powdery substance. It is highly addictive and dangerous.

Common Application – An application with which students can apply to multiple schools.

Course Registration – The period of official class selection for the upcoming quarter or semester. Prior to registration, it is best to prepare several back-up courses in case a particular class becomes full. If a course is full, students can place themselves on the waitlist, although this still does not guarantee entry.

Division Athletics – Athletic classifications range from Division I to Division III. Division IA is the most competitive, while Division III is considered to be the least competitive.

Dorm – A dorm (or dormitory) is an on-campus housing facility. Dorms can provide a range of options from suite-style rooms to more communal options that include shared bathrooms. Most first-year students live in dorms. Some upperclassmen who wish to stay on campus also choose this option.

Early Action – An application option with which a student can apply to a school and receive an early acceptance response without a binding commitment. This system is becoming less and less available.

Early Decision – An application option that students should use only if they are certain they plan to attend the school in question. If a student applies using the early decision option and is admitted, he or she is required and bound to attend that university. Admission rates are usually higher among students who apply through early decision, as the student is clearly indicating that the school is his or her first choice.

Ecstasy – An illegal drug. Also known as "E" or "X," ecstasy looks like a pill and most resembles an aspirin. Considered a party drug, ecstasy is very dangerous and can be deadly.

Ethernet – An extremely fast Internet connection available in most university-owned residence halls. To use an Ethernet connection properly, a student will need a network card and cable for his or her computer.

Fake ID – A counterfeit identification card that contains false information. Most commonly, students get fake IDs with altered birthdates so that they appear to be older than 21 (and therefore of legal drinking age). Even though it is illegal, many college students have fake IDs in hopes of purchasing alcohol or getting into bars.

Frosh – Slang for "freshman" or "freshmen."

Hazing – Initiation rituals administered by some fraternities or sororities as part of the pledging process. Many universities have outlawed hazing due to its degrading, and sometimes dangerous, nature.

Intramurals (IMs) – A popular, and usually free, sport league in which students create teams and compete against one another. These sports vary in competitiveness and can include a range of activities—everything from billiards to water polo. IM sports are a great way to meet people with similar interests.

Keg – Officially called a half-barrel, a keg contains roughly 200 12-ounce servings of beer.

LSD – An illegal drug, also known as acid, this hallucinogenic drug most commonly resembles a tab of paper.

Marijuana – An illegal drug, also known as weed or pot; along with alcohol, marijuana is one of the most commonly-found drugs on campuses across the country.

Major –The focal point of a student's college studies; a specific topic that is studied for a degree. Examples of majors include physics, English, history, computer science, economics, business, and music. Many students decide on a specific major before arriving on campus, while others are simply "undecided" until declaring a major. Those who are extremely interested in two areas can also choose to double major.

Meal Block – The equivalent of one meal. Students on a meal plan usually receive a fixed number of meals per week. Each meal, or "block," can be redeemed at the school's dining facilities in place of cash. Often, a student's weekly allotment of meal blocks will be forfeited if not used.

Minor – An additional focal point in a student's education. Often serving as a complement or addition to a student's main area of focus, a minor has fewer requirements and prerequisites to fulfill than a major. Minors are not required for graduation from most schools; however some students who want to explore many different interests choose to pursue both a major and a minor.

Mushrooms – An illegal drug. Also known as "'shrooms," this drug resembles regular mushrooms but is extremely hallucinogenic.

Off-Campus Housing – Housing from a particular landlord or rental group that is not affiliated with the university. Depending on the college, off-campus housing can range from extremely popular to non-existent. Students who choose to live off campus are typically given more freedom, but they also have to deal with possible subletting scenarios, furniture, bills, and other issues. In addition to these factors, rental prices and distance often affect a student's decision to move off campus.

Office Hours – Time that teachers set aside for students who have questions about coursework. Office hours are a good forum for students to go over any problems and to show interest in the subject material.

Pledging – The early phase of joining a fraternity or sorority, pledging takes place after a student has gone through rush and received a bid. Pledging usually lasts between one and two semesters. Once the pledging period is complete and a particular student has done everything that is required to become a member, that student is considered a brother or sister. If a fraternity or a sorority would decide to "haze" a group of students, this initiation would take place during the pledging period.

Private Institution – A school that does not use tax revenue to subsidize education costs. Private schools typically cost more than public schools and are usually smaller.

Prof – Slang for "professor."

Public Institution – A school that uses tax revenue to subsidize education costs. Public schools are often a good value for in-state residents and tend to be larger than most private colleges.

Quarter System (or Trimester System) – A type of academic calendar system. In this setup, students take classes for three academic periods. The first quarter usually starts in late September or early October and concludes right before Christmas. The second quarter usually starts around early to mid–January and finishes up around March or April. The last academic quarter, or "third quarter," usually starts in late March or early April and finishes up in late May or Mid-June. The fourth quarter is summer. The major difference between the quarter system and semester system is that students take more, less comprehensive courses under the quarter calendar.

RA (Resident Assistant) – A student leader who is assigned to a particular floor in a dormitory in order to help to the other students who live there. An RA's duties include ensuring student safety and providing assistance wherever possible.

Recitation – An extension of a specific course; a review session. Some classes, particularly large lectures, are supplemented with mandatory recitation sessions that provide a relatively personal class setting.

Rolling Admissions – A form of admissions. Most commonly found at public institutions, schools with this type of policy continue to accept students throughout the year until their class sizes are met. For example, some schools begin accepting students as early as December and will continue to do so until April or May.

Room and Board – This figure is typically the combined cost of a university-owned room and a meal plan.

Room Draw/Housing Lottery – A common way to pick on-campus room assignments for the following year. If a student decides to remain in university-owned housing, he or she is assigned a unique number that, along with seniority, is used to determine his or her housing for the next year.

Rush – The period in which students can meet the brothers and sisters of a particular chapter and find out if a given fraternity or sorority is right for them. Rushing a fraternity or a sorority is not a requirement at any school. The goal of rush is to give students who are serious about pledging a feel for what to expect.

Semester System – The most common type of academic calendar system at college campuses. This setup typically includes two semesters in a given school year. The fall semester starts around the end of August or early September and concludes before winter vacation. The spring semester usually starts in mid-January and ends in late April or May.

Student Center/Rec Center/Student Union – A common area on campus that often contains study areas, recreation facilities, and eateries. This building is often a good place to meet up with fellow students; depending on the school, the student center can have a huge role or a non-existent role in campus life.

Student ID – A university-issued photo ID that serves as a student's key to school-related functions. Some schools require students to show these cards in order to get into dorms, libraries, cafeterias, and other facilities. In addition to storing meal plan information, in some cases, a student ID can actually work as a debit card and allow students to purchase things from bookstores or local shops.

Suite – A type of dorm room. Unlike dorms that feature communal bathrooms shared by the entire floor, suites offer bathrooms shared only among the suite. Suite-style dorm rooms can house anywhere from two to ten students.

TA (Teacher's Assistant) – An undergraduate or grad student who helps in some manner with a specific course. In some cases, a TA will teach a class, assist a professor, grade assignments, or conduct office hours.

Undergraduate – A student in the process of studying for his or her bachelor's degree.

ABOUT THE AUTHOR

I always knew that someday I'd want the opportunity to write a book. However, I never expected that I would be given that opportunity by the age of 20. Being able to dig deeper into Xavier University than I ever imagined has been a learning experience, to say the least.

Aside from my personal satisfaction in compiling this guide, I also hope that those who read this publication have a better sense of what life is like at Xavier. When I was a senior in high school, my main concern was that I felt like I had no idea what I was in for once I actually arrived at school. I wished I had some sort of magical book that told me things that you couldn't learn from brochures or guided tours. I hope that for the reader, this guide to Xavier becomes that magic book that helps you make what is undoubtedly one of the most important decisions a person can make at this point in their life.

I am still astounded by the new and interesting things I am exposed to on a daily basis at Xavier. In the past few years, I've seen things and met people I would've never imagined existed while growing up in the sheltered paradise that is my home near Baltimore, MD. I guess you can't learn to fly unless you jump out of the nest. Looking back, I can honestly say I'm glad I took that leap.

As far as my background goes, I was born in raised in northern Baltimore County, Maryland. I graduated from Hereford High School and enrolled in Xavier that fall. My biggest writing influence and favorite author is F. Scott Fitzgerald. I was the senior sports writer at the Xavier University *Newswire*, where I covered basketball and published a column entitled "Dave Rants." In my free time, I enjoy playing basketball and golf, watching movies and ESPN, and taking as many naps as humanly possible.

I would also be a big moron if I didn't take this opportunity to thank some of the people who have helped me in one way or another in my infant writing career and through the composition of this guide—Mom, Dad, Dan, Holly, Robin, and the rest of the family. Thanks to everyone at XU, including Nora, Jimmy, Josh, Ryan, Bob, Rabbi, Jay, Tony, Brian, T-Bag, the Way, Nick, Coccitto, Ann, Bobby Nachos, Farsad, everyone I'm forgetting, as well as all those at the *Newswire*, especially Steve, Jackie, Lisa, the Moskos, and Dancox. Thank you to those who have supported me back east, including Kevin Cate, Ashley Boo, Bobby, Simms, Hartman, Casner, Joe, Erin, Sarah, Liz, Carrie, DiMayo, Kyle, and about a million others. And finally, thank you to everyone at College Prowler for giving an idiot college sports writer the chance of a lifetime.

This work is dedicated in loving memory to Tobias James Harring.

David Gilmore, Jr.
davidgilmore@collegeprowler.com

California Colleges

California dreamin'?
This book is a must have for you!

CALIFORNIA COLLEGES
7¼" X 10", 762 Pages Paperback
$29.95 Retail
1-59658-501-3

Stanford, UC Berkeley, Caltech—California is home
to some of America's greatest institutes of higher
learning. *California Colleges* gives the lowdown on 24
of the best, side by side, in one prodigious volume.

New England Colleges

Looking for peace in the Northeast?
Pick up this regional guide to New England!

NEW ENGLAND COLLEGES
7¼" X 10", 1015 Pages Paperback
$29.95 Retail
1-59658-504-8

New England is the birthplace of many prestigious universities, and with so many to choose from, picking the right school can be a tough decision. With inside information on over 34 competive Northeastern schools, *New England Colleges* provides the same high-quality information prospective students expect from College Prowler in one all-inclusive, easy-to-use reference.

Schools of the South

Headin' down south? This book will help you find your way to the perfect school!

SCHOOLS OF THE SOUTH
7¼" X 10", 773 Pages Paperback
$29.95 Retail
1-59658-503-X

Southern pride is always strong. Whether it's across town or across state, many Southern students are devoted to their home sweet home. *Schools of the South* offers an honest student perspective on 36 universities available south of the Mason-Dixon.

Untangling
the Ivy League

The ultimate book for everything Ivy!

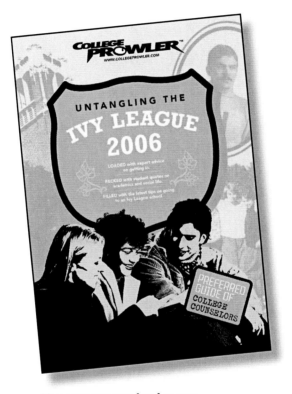

UNTANGLING THE IVY LEAGUE
7¼" X 10", 567 Pages Paperback
$24.95 Retail
1-59658-500-5

Ivy League students, alumni, admissions officers, and other top insiders get together to tell it like it is. *Untangling the Ivy League* covers every aspect—from admissions and athletics to secret societies and urban legends—of the nation's eight oldest, wealthiest, and most competitive colleges and universities.

Need Help Paying For School?

Apply for our scholarship!

College Prowler awards thousands of dollars a year to students who compose the best essays.
E-mail scholarship@collegeprowler.com for more information, or call 1-800-290-2682.

Apply now at **www.collegeprowler.com**

Tell Us What Life Is Really Like at Your School!

Have you ever wanted to let people know what your college is really like? Now's your chance to help millions of high school students choose the right college.

Let your voice be heard.

Check out *www.collegeprowler.com* for more info!

Need More Help?

Do you have more questions about this school?
Can't find a certain statistic? College Prowler is
here to help. We are the best source of college
information out there. We have a network
of thousands of students who can get the latest
information on any school to you ASAP.
E-mail us at info@collegeprowler.com with your
college-related questions.

E-Mail Us Your College-Related Questions!

Check out *www.collegeprowler.com* for more details.
1-800-290-2682

Write For Us!
Get published! Voice your opinion.

Writing a College Prowler guidebook is both fun and rewarding; our open-ended format allows your own creativity free reign. Our writers have been featured in national newspapers and have seen their names in bookstores across the country. Now is your chance to break into the publishing industry with one of the country's fastest-growing publishers!

Apply now at **www.collegeprowler.com**

Contact editor@collegeprowler.com or
call 1-800-290-2682 for more details.

Pros and Cons

Still can't figure out if this is the right school for you?
You've already read through this in-depth guide; why not
list the pros and cons? It will really help with narrowing down
your decision and determining whether or not
this school is right for you.

Pros	Cons
....	....
....	....
....	....
....	....
....	....
....	....
....	....
....	....
....	....
....	....
....	....
....	....
....	....

Pros and Cons

Still can't figure out if this is the right school for you?
You've already read through this in-depth guide; why not
list the pros and cons? It will really help with narrowing down
your decision and determining whether or not
this school is right for you.

Pros	Cons
....	....
....	....
....	....
....	....
....	....
....	....
....	....
....	....
....	....
....	....
....	....
....	....

Notes

....

....

....

....

....

....

....

....

....

....

....

....

....

Notes

Notes

....

....

....

....

....

....

....

....

....

....

....

....

....

Notes

....

....

....

....

....

....

....

....

....

....

....

....

....

Notes

....

....

....

....

....

....

....

....

....

....

....

....

....

....

Notes

....

....

....

....

....

....

....

....

....

....

....

....

....

Notes

Notes

Notes

Notes

....

....

....

....

....

....

....

....

....

....

....

....

....

Notes

....

....

....

....

....

....

....

....

....

....

....

....

....

Notes

Notes

....

....

....

....

....

....

....

....

....

....

....

....

....

....

Notes

....

....

....

....

....

....

....

....

....

....

....

....

....

Notes

....

....

....

....

....

....

....

....

....

....

....

....

....

Notes

....

....

....

....

....

....

....

....

....

....

....

....

....

Notes

Notes

....

....

....

....

....

....

....

....

....

....

....

....

....

Notes

Notes

Notes

....

....

....

....

....

....

....

....

....

....

....

....

....

Notes

....

....

....

....

....

....

....

....

....

....

....

....

....

Notes

....

....

....

....

....

....

....

....

....

....

....

....

....

Notes

Notes

....

....

....

....

....

....

....

....

....

....

....

....

....

....

Notes

....

....

....

....

....

....

....

....

....

....

....

....

....

....

Notes

....

....

....

....

....

....

....

....

....

....

....

....

....